Computer Software Evaluation:

Balancing User's Needs & Wants

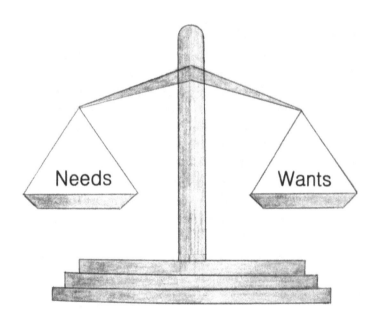

Needs

Wants

Dale Carpenter

"The Clark Kent of Librarianship"

This publication is designed to provide accurate information in regards to this specific subject matter. It is sold with the understanding that the author and publisher is not engaged in rendering legal, accounting or other professional services. If expert assistance is required, the services of a competent professional should be sought.

Published by Lies Told Press, LTD. - Non-fiction division.
Printed in the United States of America.

Lies Told Press, LTD. is a non-profit company helping authors and artists publish and market their works. All profits, except for what is needed to keep us running, go directly back to the authors and artists. Lies Told Press, LTD. books are available at www.Lulu.com.

Carpenter, Dale
Computer Software Evaluation: Balancing User's Needs & Wants
First print edition.

ISBN 978-0-9631910-7-6

1. Computer software evaluation.
2. Needs analysis.
3. Requirement analysis.
4. Project management.
5. Software selection.
6. User-center design.

HD69.P75C48   2017
658.404

Thank to David M., Sam M. and Tim P.
who kept this project from crashing on the rocks
of corporate stupidity and narrow mindedness.

Computer Software Evaluation: Balancing User's Needs & Wants

RESOURCES:

Introduction:

Several years ago I was the first Librarian hired by a small but growing pharmaceutical firm which I will call Our Company (OUR). My main task was to provide a full range of reference and information services. But since OUR did not have a 'library', it became my responsibility to create one to "archive, manage and retrieve documents ('track only versions of the official document') for OUR in a secure and controlled location, while making a document inventory available to all OUR employees via an easy-to-use interface."

This is an historical overview of the process I went through to select, gain approval for, and install a software system to manage the corporate documents for Our Company.

Now remember, I was tasked with creating the physical library, AND finding document management software to track BOTH the physical documents AND their electronic equivalents. Most software review projects do not handle all these multiple tasks at the same time.

To quickly describe the process, I met with department managers to discover what documents their groups created and worked with and what sort of regulatory and legal requirements the company had to meet. I met with the Information Technology group manager to find out what computer hardware and software the company used. This gave me the business requirements which a document management system had to meet. I electronically surveyed all company employees for their input on what the most valuable services the Library could perform. This helped me list all of the specific requirements a software system had to have to meet our business needs. After reviewing a lot of software programs, I emailed several software companies and asked them if their software would meet our detailed requirements. Once they filled out our requirement forms, I invited them in for a software demonstration. Based on how well they met our specific requirements, I selected the top performer, and presented my purchase recommendations to management.

When I mentioned doing this at meetings of the professional societies I belong to, enough people asked me for details and help on similar projects, I knew I had to write this book. I hope you find it interesting and helpful.

Prolog: Computer software evaluation based on "Needs Analysis" and "User-Centered Design"

Many times in my professional career and personal life I have had to select a product or service or I was part of a team which had to select a product or service. Sometimes it was fairly simple and many times it was very complex, based upon the needs and wants evident in the situation. Because I have done this many times I decided to share my experience in a recent situation so others doing computer software evaluation may benefit from my experience.

First a bit about my background. I have almost 40 years of experience in creating and modernizing corporate libraries in the aerospace/defense, telecommunications, executive outplacement, and pharmaceutical industries. I have worked with computer systems based on VAX, UNIX, and desktop personal software, as well as paper based systems. Some were systems created in-house specifically for the corporate Library, others modified from other computer systems, and others purchased from vendors of library software. I have a Masters of Library Science degree from SUNY Geneseo. I miss the old wooden card catalog files and hope to find some for my home.

Now let's define what we are talking about. These are my definitions and may not precisely match what other individuals or organizations may say.

Needs analysis is the process you go through when you decide to purchase a product or service. Imagine I need a new car. What I "**want**" is a 1960 era E-Type Jaguar painted British Racing Green or a 1972 Volvo 1800ES painted battleship grey. However, I currently live in the Northeast and drive between 20,000 and 25,000 miles a year including driving in New England and upstate New York in the wintertime. I canoe, wilderness camp and car camp. I am a fly fisherman and do not want to have to take apart my fly rod when driving from one spot on a stream to another. I love to go garage sailing and buy odd things.

So you can see what I **need** is a vehicle which will meet my requirements. It should have all-wheel or 4-wheel drive for those drives in wintertime and a lot of lockable storage space. A pickup truck would be nice but I would have to put a top over the bed and I could not reach items in the back without climbing out of the cab and opening the tailgate. The gas mileage needs to be also considered and a station wagon usually gets better mileage than a truck or van. So a station wagon best fits my needs, which is why I have owned various station wagons for over 30 years.

User-centered design is just that process. Defining who the users are, defining their goals and tasks, what information and functions they want and really need from any product or system, and understanding how those users think the product or system should work. Imagine an architect sitting down with a family and talking with them about the custom house they want built. Depending on the size and lifestyle of the family they will have certain needs and wants. The architect will try to determine how the family will live and play in the house and design it to meet or exceed their needs (number of bedrooms and bathrooms, size of kitchen, etc.), and their wants (do they want a music or game room, etc.).

Requirement analysis is the process of determining the existing needs and or the conditions that must be met for a new product or service. Usually this focuses on what software and hardware is currently being used in house and making sure the considered product or service is compatible with them.

Project management is the activity and process undertaken to achieve specific goals. It has a defined beginning and end and usually restrictions on time and money. Usually the desired end result is also well defined. You could consider the writing of this book as an exercise in project management. I know what I want the end result to be, I know when I want it finished and I know what it will take to get it done.

A steering committee is responsible for monitoring a project and making sure it complies with the defined restrictions and is online to meet the specific goals. It usually consist of members from the various groups or departments which the project will affect.

What follows are my steps in this process to determine OUR employee's needs and wants, find a software program which fulfilled them and bring it in house.

Software Evaluation and Selection Process

Learn about company and industry

Draft plan and process options

Create info audits

Interview with main process owners

Information survey of groups which will use the system

Create list of functional requirements by rewriting critical needs from user surveys

Group desired requirements

Draw screen layouts showing functional requirements

Create steering committee of main process owners

Draft department policies and operating procedures for handling of documents

View known vendor sites with functional requirements in hand

Search websites and directories for other systems

Mail requirements document to vendors

Create spreadsheet with value weighting for comparisons of systems

Populate spreadsheet with vendor's filled out requirements document

Invite vendors in to give demos

Send out Requests For Proposal

Create proposal for software selection

Present proposal to steering committee

Get steering committee approval

Create capital expenditure request

Present capital expenditure request to management

Get management approval of capital expenditure

Get management signoff on capital expenditure

Install and run software

Give user training

Roll out system to one group

Use feedback from first group to modify system and/or training

Roll out system to all groups

Chapter 1 - Learn about the Company and the Industry

Learn as much as you can about the company and the industry, especially if you are new to that industry.

You will need to draw extensively on your manager's knowledge of the company and the people who work there. Who will support your efforts to bring in a document management software system, who opposes it, and who doesn't care? Your manager may be able to give you information on the best ways to approach individuals and what their work habits are which will be useful in deciding ways in which to influence them.

My manager, the Vice-President of Information Technology, said one of the biggest opponents would be the Director of Information Management. This person was a chemist who had taken on the task of doing scientific research for the company in the years before I was hired. They thought everything could and should be done with Microsoft SharePoint (2002 version). They reported to the VP of Business Infrastructure, a person who just wanted everyone to get along.

Being new to the pharmaceutical industry was a benefit in several ways. I could plead ignorance while asking all sorts of questions about how things were done and why they were done that way. I could ask people to compare the processes used at their former employees, mostly large pharma companies, to the processes at OUR and ask them which process they thought were best and how to improve the processes. I could mention processes from other industries and ask for opinions on if this might be a better way of doing things. If I had had experience in the pharmaceutical industry, people would have assumed I knew how to do things and would not have granted me as much freedom.

A great help were presentations on the drug development process and the role of the Food and Drug Administration (FDA) in the regulatory process. These presentations had been developed in-house for continuing education courses taught by various department managers. Each department would talk about their role in the company and how they helped bring the drugs to market. Attendance at these courses was required and was a great way to learn about all aspects of the company and meet the employees.

We did have a file room where all the regulatory documents were stored. It was wide open with no sign-in or sign-out process, allowing anyone to walk off with documents. Often people had to go wandering around, asking who had a certain document. This chaos was good because it was apparent to almost everyone that more control had to be placed over the documents. The bad part of having a pre-existing library was the 'owners' who were responsible for it did not want to give it up.

This is the first draft of my plan for building the new library. Notice how I was covering everything from high level issues such as inter-departmental relationships down to the nitty-gritty details of how the classification system should work. This was drafted to show my manager, the VP of IT, how I was planning to work through the process.

Building Our Company's Corporate Library

1. **First** consult with key members of teams/departments to ensure all business requirements are documented –
   a. identify what regulatory documents will need to be filed and maintained
   b. identify what company/department documents will need to be filed and maintained
   c. identify what documents will be brought to Homebase from other locations
   d. identify the major document types
   e. identify requirements (legal, regulatory, retention, etc.) for document types

2. **Next** design business requirements into a solution, in line with company strategic aims, policies and procedures -
   a. document to be 'view' only unless permission granted by head of department which owns document
   b. all changes or modifications to documents will be tracked by software
   c. originators will have final sign-off on all content of documents
   d. certain documents will be viewed only by the department which owns that document, i.e. Sales and ad agreements, contracts, legal, etc.
   e. templates for company forms and documents available to all
   f. creation of Library SOPs

g. document filing and retrieval method

h. document control methods (check-in, check-out etc.) including version control

i. document archiving and retention procedure (includes legal requirements for each document type and solutions for security of documents)

3. **Then** implement design solution in agreement with infrastructure and resources -

    a. classification solution (developed in-house or purchased from outside vendor) must co-exist seamlessly with current OUR software

    b. training sessions on Library system will be developed and presented to OUR employees so they may learn to use the system to access documents

    c. what software packages is the company using now for information and documentation both structured and unstructured?

4. **Finally** manage Library to ensure -

    a. regulatory requirements are met;

    b. ensure return on investment;

    c. productivity and performance measures are met;

    d. overall customer satisfaction is realized

5. Any plan has to address these essential processes:

    a. identify and capture relevant knowledge

    b. store, organize and classify information in a central repository

    c. provide knowledge to users thru easy automated access

    d. interact with knowledge and users creating a feedback loop to beginning (number 5a)

The following will need to be answered by company employees because these issues will affect how the Library can protect the documents it is responsible for. A number of these items became points of discussion for the Steering Committee.

Questions and Issues which affect Selection of Software and Management of Documents

1. OUR organizational chart is needed so I may meet with department heads and group managers.
      a. introduce myself and offer whatever help I can to assist them in their jobs
      b. learn what they do and how they do it
      c. learn what information they create and how it is used
      d. learn what information they need to function and where and how they obtain that info
      e. find out if they have and use a classification scheme for department documents

2. A procedure is needed which mandates all departments to provide Library with those documents required for the regulatory process and auditing process.
      a. how do we determine what documents these are?
      b. how do we determine what version of document is required?
      c. keep only final, or all versions?
      d. how can we be sure Library receives all documents from every department?

3. These other procedures will be needed:
      a. procedure detailing process by which Library receives, classifies, securely stores, retains, and provides knowledge of (database or index) and access to (sign-out), company and external documents and records.
      b. procedure detailing how Library provides access to documents – sign-out procedure
      c. procedure detailing records retention and archiving by Library, either in house or off site
      e. Policy and SOP updating procedure
      f. disaster recovery plan

4. Are we concerned with only paper documents or both paper and electronic forms of documents?
   - a. if electronic version, how do we maintain access control?
   - b. done thru Microsoft SharePoint?

5. Classification system should include any existing department classification system which will be placed into a searchable subfield. Create taxonomy in-house or purchase from outside source?

6. Storage space must be secure and restricted to Library staff only.

7. Library must provide to OUR a searchable electronic database and index of holdings.
   - a. how?
   - b. thru SharePoint?
   - c. searchable by what terms? and to what depth? (full text?)
   - d. ability to request documents thru database?

8. How does Library provide access to the documents when required by staff?
   - a. do we provide the original or a copy?
   - b. do we provide a paper or electronic version?

9. How do we determine the retention schedule for each item?
   - a. by department procedures, by market lifetime of the product, or regulatory requirements?

10. How does a OUR employee request access to a document?
   - a. by paper form, email, electronic form?

11. How long will an employee be able to sign a document out of the Library?
   - a. how do we enforce this?

12. Will we need to retain sign-out forms showing who looked at what document? (This is a good idea.)
   - a. how long will we have to retain sign-out forms?

13. How do we determine if an employee has the right to view a document?
   - a. by SharePoint reader/author/approver/coordinator function?
   - b. or by department manager approval?

14. What level of detail must the classification scheme show?

      a. more levels of detail the better storage & retrieval but more detail adds more work

      b. must we go down to table of contents level as shown in Standard Operating Procedure OUR-CL-002 addendum?

15. What departments have functions which may overlap the document control function or have functions which might become the Librarian's responsibility?

      a. Who are they, where are they, what do they do?

      b. Knowledge Management

      c. Medical Affairs Information

      d. others?

Right away I realized most classification systems (Dewey, Library of Congress, etc.) were not precise enough to deal with internal company documents. I asked the Pharmaceutical and Biotechnical Division of the Special Libraries Association (SLA) if anyone knew of a system that would work but received no helpful answers. I assumed no one was able to share any company system that had been created internally.

Classification Scheme must cover these items and answer these questions to be useful:

What falls into my area of responsibility? (What else will be my responsibility? Research, document acquisition and delivery, etc.?)

Three main classes of documents:
1. Documents published in-house – 3 types:
        regulatory documents – required for regulatory approval
        external documents – created for external release, (marketing or sales materials)
        internal documents – policies, procedures, memos, etc.
2. Documents received from outside sources
        clinical study materials
3. Reference materials purchased for in-house use: Are they held by departments or individuals?

Documents created in house: (VP of IT says company policy is "paper copies are the official copy"). Questions to ask during info audits of process owners.
        What are they?
        Who creates them and who owns them?
        How are they used and by whom?
        How often are they used or accessed? Does this change over time?
        What regulatory requirements pertain to them, i.e. retention period, original copy, paper or electronic?
        Is version control needed?
        Is access control needed?
        Are they available in paper or electronic format (Internet, databases, CD-ROM, email) or both?
        Are they stored in paper or electronic format or both?
        How long do they need to be retained?
        Do they need to be in the Library?

Documents or reference materials received from outside sources:
        What are they?
        Where do we obtain them?
        Who obtains them for company or department?
        How are they used and by whom?
        Are they shared among departments?
        How often are they used or accessed? Does this change over
time?
        What are regulatory requirements for keeping these items?
Do we need to obtain updated versions on a regular basis?
        Is version control needed?
        Is access control needed?
        Are they available in paper or electronic format (Internet,
databases, CD-ROM, email) or both?
        Are they stored in paper or electronic format or both?
        How long do they need to be retained?
        Do they need to be in the Library?

FIELDS NEEDED IN CLASSIFICATION – should be searchable -

Document source
Title
Study name
Study number/amendment/supplement
Date
Author(s)
Country(s)
State(s)
Hospital(s)
Number of pages
Number of volumes
Agency form # (i.e. FDA 3397)
Subject
Product name: chemical name, trial name, trade name, generic name
Keywords
Table of contents
Existing department classification code
Version number
Which version number is official legal copy?
Frequency of updates
Retention period
Date of document for retention calculation

Related documents in process
Indication of content subject to regulatory compliance
Company confidentiality
Information which potentially could be used in identity theft or company fraud
Publisher
Notes
ISBN
Location within facility

Possible Classification Scheme – draft
Tracked by Product (chemical name, trial name, trade name, generic) and by Time

ACQUISITION OF PRODUCT - materials relating to identification and acquisition by OUR Company

Investigational New Drug (IND) – materials relating to the time period of study trials
- protocols
- reports
Clinical study numbers 1 to ?
- synopsis
- study report
- data listing
- publications

New Drug Application (NDA) – materials relating to submission of drug and passage thru regulatory process

NDA submission
- manufacturing
- safety
- investigation
- protocols
- study reports
- statistical data
- administrative
- quality
- clinical
- labeling
- chemistry
investigative information
promotional materials
correspondence - Dear Doctor letters, etc.
annual reports
- periodic Safety Adverse Events (SAE)
safety information - Medwatch
protocols
trial master file
- contracts
- ERB approval letters
- electronic signature forms

- signature pages

MARKETING of PRODUCT – materials relating to period of time drug is on the market
Food and Drug Administration (FDA) requirements

All other materials

Chapter 2 - Draft Plan and Process Options

I drafted options for software solutions for the library. The bare bones option was for me to use a yellow legal pad and a pencil for inventory and circulation tasks. One step up from that would be to use a computer spreadsheet such as Microsoft Excel as an inventory and circulation system. These were quickly discarded because they offered no ability for other employees to search for items.

Plan options for library

The time it takes to input document data into any library system must be taken into account when determining how quickly a system can be made useful and available. This may be decreased if using automated data form capture software or electronically scanned documents are table or full-text indexed. Both of these options add to the cost of implementing a library system.

Whatever system is developed or purchased must be seamlessly compatible with current company software systems, if any.

Basic:

Build library software database in-house – this might use Access to store data, Visual Basic to drive all database forms and some type of software (Crystal Report?) to create and manage the input screens/forms and the search screens/forms

    Plus: low cost, we build a database customized for our needs, in-house IT support,

    Minus: time to build database and ensure it functions as we desire, database won't have certain capabilities (i.e., barcode reading, Boolean logic searching, retention & archiving tracking, full-text searching, etc.) IT staff spending time on creation and upkeep,

    Unknown: will database be able to handle increasing demands as company grows? How much time will it take IT for development, implementation and support of database? will it ensure coverage of all regulatory requirements?

Midrange:

Purchase library package from outside vendor which performs library administrative functions and basic document control management
Plus: quick implementation and operation after purchase of system, support from vendor, multiple capabilities we need (based on info audits and user survey),
Minus: purchase cost and annual support costs, learning curve for staff and users, off-site support,
Unknown: functionality with OUR software systems (SharePoint, etc.)? will system be able to handle increasing demands as company grows? will it ensure coverage of all regulatory requirements?

Top end:

Purchase library package from outside vendor that performs library administrative functions, document control management and imaging functions
Plus: quick implementation and operation after purchase of system, support from vendor, multiple capabilities including electronic access to and control of documents, easy creation of backup files for disaster recovery (off site storage), space savings (electronic instead of paper documents in-house),
Minus: purchase cost and annual support costs, learning curve for staff and users, off-site support, time to scan documents into system,
Unknown: functionality with OUR software systems (SharePoint, etc.)? cost and time if system vendor does scanning, will it ensure coverage of all regulatory requirements?

I researched specific needs of the pharmaceutical industry, regulations, requirements, etc., by asking process owners during the info audit what they were and by asking for input from other professionals in the industry. I also went to the government agencies that regulate the industry and searched their websites for information.

I emailed the listserv of the Pharmaceutical and Biotechnical Division asking if anyone could help me by pointing to the specific requirements of certain regulatory agencies. No one responded with specific enough information to be useful. I found most of what I needed and used from OUR department managers.

It quickly became apparent almost everyone wanted me to focus only on OUR Company regulatory documents and nothing else. This was a high priority in case we ever were audited. My manager told me this was the major factor in creating the Library and the corporate librarian position. Everyone else was too busy to take on the task or did not want it. Upper management realized the control of the documents needed to be one person's responsibility and not become an issue to be fought over. Most of the company were quite busy creating documents and did not want to have to deal with the day to day activities of document control.

As my manager said *"The basic function of the Library will be to archive, manage and retrieve documents ('track only versions of the official document') for OUR in a secure and controlled location, while making an inventory of the documents available to all employees of OUR with an easy-to-use interface."*

This quote was extremely helpful in focusing everyone's attention on the specific issues at hand whenever discussions tended to start wandering into different issues.

Chapter 3 - Create Info Audits and Talk with Main Process Owners

Perform information audits with the main process owners (department managers, etc.) to learn their specific needs, wants, and work processes. This will help you to get to know people, as well as learn about specific requirements those people have or which might exist in the company or industry. These requirements might pertain to company classified or regulated or government classified or regulated documents.

> Info audits should find out:
> - Where info & data comes from, what is done with it and where does it go?
> - Who does info come from, what do they do with it and who does it go to?
> - How many different types of documents, books, periodicals, articles, etc.; how many total; what format will things be in; how often accessed; etc.
> - Is there any data or info migration from an older system or another system to be done?

(Having no existing system turned out to be a positive factor because many software vendors charge a large amount for data conversion from an existing system to their system. In my experience, most data conversion can be done by patient trial and error after you learn a new system.)

These are the groups within OUR and the types of documents and materials they create internally. All groups create corporate Policies, Standard Operating Procedures (SOPs) and Work Instructions. Other documents are listed after the group name. (Initially, I was told this is what each group created. I found out ALL groups produce a lot more material but they do not want anyone else handling or controlling it.)

Biostatistics:

Business Development:

Clinical:
        Clinical trial materials

Communications:
- Media releases
- Slide sets

Corporate:

Data Management:

Finance:
- Quarterly and annual reports
- SEC filings
- Contracts

Human Resources:
- Performance evaluations
- Quarterly and annual reports
- Employee handbook

Information Technology:

Legal:
- Contracts
- Confidentiality agreements
- Trade marks
- Licensing agreements

Manufacturing:
- Manufacturing records
- Specifications and methods
- Bills of materials
- Data sheets
- Engineering drawings
- Good laboratory practices
- Protection of workers

Marketing:
- Strategic brand plan
- Sales force communications
- Creative briefs
- Position papers
- Tactical plans
- Sales training manuals
- Medical information letters

Advertising
Pricing and reimbursement

Product Quality:
Regulatory submissions
Requests for quotations from contractors
Requests for information from contractors
Contracts
Forecasts (spreadsheets)
Gantt charts
Reports from contractors

Quality Assurance:
Periodic stability reports
Annual product review
Supplier qualification reports
Quality/technical agreements
Internal audit reports
Deviations
Specifications
Product compliant investigations

Regulatory:
Protocols
Informed consent
Informed consent waiver
Case report forms
Study reports
Integrated safety summary (per CTD?)
Integrated efficacy summary (per CTD?)
FDA cover letters
Investigator's brochure
HIPAA waiver
Other waivers
Sub-study documents
Site initiation visit memo/form
Study monitoring visit memo/form
Study site close-out memo/form
NDA quarterly safety reports
NDA annual report
IND annual report
Package inserts
NDA details

NDA summaries

Safety:
    Training records

Training:
    Training materials
    Training records

This is the formal email request I sent to each process owner when I asked for a meeting.

> I need to find out how information is created, moves and is used within Our Company so when the company library is created, it meets regulatory requirements, ensures return on investment and provides overall customer satisfaction. Since you are one of the main sequence process owners, could we please set up a time to meet? If you are very busy this week and next, perhaps you could suggest a key member of your department who could meet with me.
>
> Dale Carpenter MLS
> Corporate Librarian
> Our Company
> A Scenic Drive
> Homebase, PA 01023
> 111-111-1111
> dale.carpenter@ourcompany.com
>
>
> These are the issues I am interested in:
>
> I need to meet with department heads and group managers:
> a. learn what they do and how they do it
> b. learn what they create and how it is used (in relation to regulatory documents)
> c. learn what information is used (in relation to regulatory documents)
> d. where and how that info is obtained (in relation to regulatory documents)
> e. does a classification scheme exist for department documents (in relation to regulatory documents)

f.   what library function or functions would provide the greatest return to you and your department?

Find the documents created in house:

What are they?

Who creates them and who owns them?

How are they used and by whom?

How often are they used or accessed? Does this change over time?

What regulatory requirements pertain to them, i.e. retention period, original copy, paper or electronic?

Is version control needed?

Is access control needed?

Are they available in paper or electronic format (Internet, databases, CD-ROM, email) or both?

Are they stored in paper or electronic format or both?

What software systems are used to create, maintain and store the documents?

How long do they need to be retained?

Do they need to be in the Library?

I created a form to capture the process owner's answers. I used this to capture answers in real time; read back what I had written to get immediate feedback from the interviewer; and also capture my personal impressions about them as a person.

NAME:
DEPT:
This discussion is primarily concerned with the legislative, audit, quality, regulatory and corporate requirements to maintain and preserve access to corporate information.

What documents are created in house?

Who creates them and who owns them?

Where do you obtain the information to create the documents?

How are they used and by whom?

How often are they used or accessed? Does this change over time?

What regulatory requirements pertain to them, i.e. retention period, original copy, paper or electronic?

Have you written formal retention policies for your documents?

Is version control needed?

Is access control needed?

What format are your documents in? (paper, electronic format (Internet, databases, CD-ROM, email), both or all?

Are they stored in paper or electronic format or both?

Are your paper records and electronic documents managed in separate systems?

What software systems are used to create, maintain and store the documents?

Do they need to be in the Library?

Does your department create or use any other information or materials we have not discussed?

Roughly, by your estimate, how many documents does your department control?
In regulatory area: all others:

Where you worked before, did they have a corporate Library? Did you use it and what use did you make of it?

What expectations do you have of the Library?

What Library function or functions would provide the "greatest return" to you and your department?

After each info audit, I put all the answers into a document, and emailed the document to the process owner saying "This is what I got from the meeting. Is this correct? Did I miss something, or write something down incorrectly? Please correct and respond." In this way, I let them know I was studious in my info gathering. I also had proof so if in the future they disputed anything, I could pull up the email and ask them why they didn't say something at the time of the interview. In one meeting I was showing quotes from the audit interviews to support my efforts and one manager denied ever saying that quote. I pulled up my notes from the meeting with him and showed the exact quote.

For the "greatest return" question, here are the answers and the department which gave them:

LIBRARY FUNCTIONS ROI

What Library function or functions would provide the greatest return to you and your department?

To **archive, manage and retrieve** documents ('track only versions of the official document') for OUR in a secure and controlled location, while making an inventory of the documents available to all employees of OUR. VP of IT (my manager)

32

Making **access** to the paper documents retained in the library as painless as possible. Compliance

Keeping GMP and compliance documents in a secure location **easily accessible** in the event of an FDA visit. Manufacturing

Storing department documents in a secure area, and having them **organized** in a logical, easy to understand manner so I may find them right away when I need them. Drug Development First Product

Having a person who **knows where things are** to cut down the hassle of finding items. Drug Safety

Controlled **access** to employee records. Human Resources

Secure retention of documents including security layering so department personnel can quickly and easily obtain needed documents when required but no one else may **access** the regulatory documents. Regulatory

Storage and access control (both here and off-site) of finance and legal documents such as tax returns, vendor payable files and the employee expense reports with receipts would be a valuable function of the Library. Chief Finance Officer (CFO)

Control and storage of documents during the trials. First Drug Program Manager

Manage the **compliance functions**, which include but are not limited to: company policies and SOPs. Chief Finance Officer (CFO)

All contracts need to be in a **central database** controlled by a contract administration owner, who would create financial summaries for auditing and financial accruing purposes. This includes GPOs, partner agreements, licensing agreements, manufacturing agreements, marketing contracts, and clinical contracts. Controller

Our group also is involved with the paying of invoices and would appreciate a **system of tracking** and paying the invoices. (would have to be linked with the Finance group). Drug Safety

Our group is very good at tracking major items but not perfect at **tracking** and capturing the day-to-day minute items. A system or process which would do this would be very valuable. Regulatory

An **integrated data warehouse** would be very useful as a repository for all data from a project or trial. This would ensure all data, no matter what format it was in, could be located and accessed when needed. First Drug Clinical Trial Manager

For due diligence requests, a "**virtual data room**" holding the documents which are usually requested would be a time and money saver. Controller, Legal

Having the drug development data we obtain from the licensing company accessible **in electronic form** for use by company departments such as Regulatory and Publications. Business Development

Having as many documents as possible available and accessible in **an electronic format.** Compliance

Ability to have documents **imaged** would be a time and money saver, as in the case of a due diligence request from an outside firm. Controller

Imaging of documents would be a very nice thing to have available. Legal

Online access to information and **periodicals**. Business Development

Electronic access to information and **periodicals**. Corporate Communications

Create guidelines for corporate wide folder and file **naming protocols** to enable easier access to and retrieval of information. Corporate Communications

Help in determining a standard practice for **naming of files** and folders to assist in name and version control. First Drug Product Manager

A company policy or system for **document naming and filing**, so everyone would know how to name and where to file documents. This would greatly speed document retrieval. Medical Affairs

A **document classification** system easily understood by everyone in the organization. Compliance

Participate in the creation and management of a **disaster recovery plan** for the company. CFO

Submissions, no matter by what department, belong together. Regulatory

Any non-internal QA report belongs with the regulatory materials. Regulatory

The more detail the library **cataloging** database contains, the more helpful it would be in finding and retrieving documents. Regulatory, Drug Safety

Chapter 4 - Info Survey of the Entire Company

This survey was created to acquire information on how the company's employee's use, handle, and are affected by paper and electronic documents. It was sent to all company employees, at that time less than 200 people. In a much larger company I would only survey those groups most directly affected by the Library's work.

Document Management Questionnaire

Which function best describes your area of focus? Please choose one.

Biostatistics
Business Development
Corporate
Communications
Data Management
Document Management
Finance/Accounting
Human Resources
Information Technology
Legal
Manufacturing
Marketing
Medical Information
Product Development
Quality Assurance
Regulatory
Risk Management
Safety
Sales
Training
Other:_____

Do you send hard copy documents to:
Biostatistics
Business Development
Corporate
Communications

Data Management
Document Management
Finance/Accounting
Human Resources
Information Technology
Legal
Manufacturing
Marketing
Medical Information
Product Development
Quality Assurance
Regulatory
Risk Management
Safety
Sales
Training
Other: _____

Do you receive hard copy document from:
Biostatistics
Business Development
Corporate
Communications
Data Management
Document Management
Finance/Accounting
Human Resources
Information Technology
Legal
Manufacturing
Marketing
Medical Information
Product Development
Quality Assurance
Regulatory
Risk Management
Safety
Sales
Training
Other: _____

Do you send emails and electronic documents/records to:
Biostatistics
Business Development
Corporate
Communications
Data Management
Document Management
Finance/Accounting
Human Resources
Information Technology
Legal
Manufacturing
Marketing
Medical Information
Product Development
Quality Assurance
Regulatory
Risk Management
Safety
Sales
Training
Other:_____

Do you receive emails and electronic documents/records from:
Biostatistics
Business Development
Corporate
Communications
Data Management
Document Management
Finance/Accounting
Human Resources
Information Technology
Legal
Manufacturing
Marketing
Medical Information
Product Development
Quality Assurance
Regulatory
Risk Management
Safety
Sales

Training
Other: _____

Are some of your paper documents duplicated?
Yes   no   not sure

Are some of your electronic documents duplicated?

Are both paper and electronic documents duplicated?

Do you have a filing system for paper documents?
Yes   no   not sure

Do you have a filing system for electronic documents?
Yes   no   not sure

Do you have a filing system for email?
Yes   no   not sure

How often do you find that a paper document is not available?
More than 3 times a day   2 to 3 times a day   daily   weekly
monthly   less often

How often do you find that an electronic document is not available?
More than 3 times a day   2 to 3 times a day   daily   weekly
monthly   less often

How often do you find that an email is not available?
More than 3 times a day   2 to 3 times a day   daily   weekly
monthly   less often

How much time per day do you spend looking for paper documents?
Very little   15 minutes or so   15 to 30 minutes   30 to 60
minutes   over 1 hour

How much time per day do you spend looking for electronic
documents?
Very little   15 minutes or so   15 to 30 minutes   30 to 60
minutes   over 1 hour

How much time per day do you spend looking for email?
Very little   15 minutes or so   15 to 30 minutes   30 to 60
minutes   over 1 hour

Do other people need or have access to your paper documents?
Yes   no   not sure

If other people do need or have access to your paper documents, how often do they need it?
Daily   weekly   monthly   quarterly   yearly   less often

Do other people need or have access to your electronic documents?
Yes   no   not sure

If other people do need or have access to your electronic documents, how often do they need it?
Daily   weekly   monthly   quarterly   yearly   less often

Do other people need or have access to your email?
Yes   no   not sure

If other people do need or have access to your email, how often do they need it?
Daily   weekly   monthly   quarterly   yearly   less often

Do you have a retention schedule or policy for paper documents?
Yes   no   not sure

Do you have a retention schedule or policy for electronic documents?
Yes   no   not sure

Do you have a retention schedule or policy for email?
Yes   no   not sure

Are you aware of any specific company policy for document retention?
Yes   no   not sure

Are you aware of any retention regulations or requirements?
Yes   no   not sure

How often do you purge paper documents?
Daily   weekly   monthly   quarterly   yearly   when out of space   never

How often do you purge electronic documents?
Daily   weekly   monthly   quarterly   yearly   when out of space   never

How often do you purge email?
Daily   weekly   monthly   quarterly   yearly   when out
of space   never

What percentage of paper documents in your work group are more
than three years old?
0-25%   25-50%   50-75%   75-100%   not sure

How often do you access paper documents that are more than three
years old?
Daily   weekly   monthly   quarterly   yearly   less often
never

What percentage of electronic documents in your work group are
more than three years old?
0-25%   25-50%   50-75%   75-100%   not sure

How often do you access electronic documents that are more than
three years old?
Daily   weekly   monthly   quarterly   yearly   less often
never

What percentage of email in your work group are more than three
years old?
0-25%   25-50%   50-75%   75-100%   not sure

How often do you access email that is more than three years old?
Daily   weekly   monthly   quarterly   yearly   less often
never

Does your work group have documents in storage?
Yes   no   not sure

If yes, do you have a list of these documents?
Yes   no   not sure

If your work group has documents in storage, how often do you
access them?
Daily   weekly   monthly   quarterly   yearly   less often
never

Does your company or work group have formal procedures on the handling, storage and/or retention of paper documents?
Yes   no   not sure

Does your company or work group have formal procedures on the handling, storage and/or retention of electronic documents?
Yes   no   not sure

Does your company or work group have formal procedures on the handling, storage and/or retention of email?
Yes   no   not sure

Is there a specific individual in your company or work group responsible for the management of documents?
Yes   no   not sure

If yes, who is this individual?

What percentages of your documents are in both paper and electronic formats?
0-25%   25-50%   50-75%   75-100%

Does your work group have a centralized storage or file system for paper documents?
Yes   no   not sure

Does your work group have a centralized storage or file system for electronic documents?
Yes   no   not sure

Does your work group have a centralized storage or file system for email?
Yes   no   not sure

What percentage of your email do you print out?
0-25%   25-50%   50-75%   75-100%

What percentage of your printed out email do you file?
0-25%   25-50%   50-75%   75-100%

Do you use your email inboxes and folders as a document storage system?
Yes   no   not sure

In an electronic document management system, how important would you rate the following functions?

	Very Important	Important	Somewhat important	Not very important	Not at all important
Sharing documents					
Indexing documents					
Document workflow					
Check-in and check-out of documents					
Automated purging of documents					

After receiving the survey responses, I created an Excel worksheet and entered the results. This provided a way of measuring, by company departments, how they were working with paper and electronic documents and what they felt were the important issues and functions a document management system should handle.

Next I surveyed company employees asking about needs, wants, and any previous experience with other systems. Part of the surveys I sent out asked if any users had knowledge of or would suggest a system. Since many of our employees had previously worked for large pharma companies, they mentioned software systems used by large corporate libraries. All of the systems mentioned were too big and expensive for what we desired to do.

This user survey was sent in an electronic format with check boxes so people could respond electronically through email.

If I do this again, I will send out only the first section of the survey and ask for volunteers to fill out a more complete survey dealing with specific functions. I heard many people were overwhelmed by the complexity of the entire survey.

User Survey on Key Features for the New Library Software

For each survey item, please select the appropriate response.

Which function best describes your area of focus? Please choose one.

Biostatistics
Business Development
Corporate
Communications
Data Management
Document Management
Finance/Accounting
Human Resources
Information Technology
Legal
Manufacturing
Marketing
Medical Information
Product Development
Quality Assurance
Regulatory
Risk Management
Safety
Sales
Training
Other: _____

Several deficiencies with our current document control system include:

- Concern if regulatory and legal requirements are being met
- Unable to find a document
- Not knowing if a document is available
- Unsure which is the most current or the final version of a document
- Material available only in a paper format
- Having related documents from a project in several locations
- Having project information in several formats; Word, Excel, email

Are there other deficiencies that especially frustrate you? Please specify.

- _____
- _____
- _____

We believe that any document control system must support the following basic functions so you may easily find what you are looking for. Please tell us how important each function is to you in your use by circling the number closest to how you feel about the category.

Searching by words in titles, authors, subjects, etc.
Crucial   Nice to Have   Not Important to me
5   4   3   2   1   0

Combination searches such as combining author and title
Crucial   Nice to Have   Not Important to me
5   4   3   2   1   0

Searching titles, authors, and subjects by exact beginning, such as author's last name
Crucial   Nice to Have   Not Important to me
5   4   3   2   1   0

Searching by document report number
Crucial   Nice to Have   Not Important to me
5   4   3   2   1   0

Ability to limit searches by location, date, and format
Crucial   Nice to Have   Not Important to me
5   4   3   2   1   0

Ability to re-sort search results in author, title, or date order
Crucial   Nice to Have   Not Important to me
5   4   3   2   1   0

Saving searches for download, email, print
Crucial   Nice to Have   Not Important to me
5   4   3   2   1   0

Email notices for document requests, recalls, overdues, etc.
Crucial   Nice to Have   Not Important to me
5   4   3   2   1   0

Hot links within the record to electronic versions of the same
title
Crucial   Nice to Have   Not Important to me
5   4   3   2   1   0

Are there any other basic functions that you think are crucial? Please
specify and tell us how important it is to you.

- _____
Crucial   Nice to Have   Not Important to me
5   4   3   2   1   0

- _____
Crucial   Nice to Have   Not Important to me
5   4   3   2   1   0

- _____
Crucial   Nice to Have   Not Important to me
5   4   3   2   1   0

Systems can implement the prior functions in different ways. Below
are detailed questions about some significant differences we've
observed in systems being used in other libraries. Please review
these questions and give us your feedback on any areas that interest
you.

**Complex User Survey on Key Features for the New Library
Software**

Title Searching: For each feature, please tell us how important it is to
you that this feature be available.

1. I can search for a word or words anywhere in a title (for example, I
do a title search for 'childhood assessment' and get both Assessment
in Early Childhood and Childhood Assessment Methods)
Crucial   Nice to Have   Don't Care/No Opinion   Would NOT Want
2   1   0   -1

2. I can search for an exact document or article title and get a list of titles that begin with the words I entered (for example, I can search for 'Science' and retrieve works entitled Science, Science Abstracts, and Science and Art)

Crucial   Nice to Have   Don't Care/No Opinion   Would NOT Want
   2   1   0   -1

3. I can search for a complete document or article title and retrieve only works with that specific title (for example, I can search for 'Science' and retrieve only works entitled Science and not also Science Abstracts or Science and Art)

Crucial   Nice to Have   Don't Care/No Opinion   Would NOT Want
   2   1   0   -1

4. If my search produces a list of series title entries with numbers in them, the numbers display in true numeric order (for example, Advances in Medicine v10 files AFTER Advances in Medicine v9)

Crucial   Nice to Have   Don't Care/No Opinion   Would NOT Want
   2   1   0   -1

5. When you search for titles, do you prefer to see a list of records immediately? Or do you prefer to see an alphabetic list of titles such as:
Design [16 titles]
Design After Dark [1 title]
Design Against Fatigue [1 title]
Etc.
from which you select a title and then see records?

- Would usually prefer to see a list of records immediately
- Would usually prefer to see an alphabetic list of titles, select a title, and then see the record or records with that title
- Have no strong preference

Author Searching: For each feature, please tell us how important it is to you that this feature be available.

6. I can search for a word or words anywhere in an author name, in any order, with or without a comma (for example, I do an author search for 'Mike Chrzan' or 'Chrzan Mike' or 'Chrzan, Mike' and get all books by Mike Chrzan)

Crucial   Nice to Have   Don't Care/No Opinion   Would NOT Want
   2   1   0   -1

7. I can search for an exact author and get a list of author names that begin with the words I entered (for example, I can search for 'Chrzan, m' and get a list of names that includes Chrzan, Mike and Chrzan, Morris but not Le Boeuf, Chrzan M.)

Crucial   Nice to Have   Don't Care/No Opinion   Would NOT Want
   2   1   0   -1

8. When you search for authors, do you prefer to see a list of records immediately? Or do you prefer to see an alphabetic list of author names such as:

Chrzan, Charles, 1726-1814 [29 titles]
Chrzan, Edward Francis, 1760-1848 [10 titles]
Chrzan, Mike, 1752-1840 [99 titles]
Etc.
from which you select a name and then see records?

- Would usually prefer to see a list of records immediately
- Would usually prefer to see an alphabetic list of author names, select an author, and then see the record or records with that author
- Have no strong preference

Subject Searching: For each feature, please tell us how important it is to you that this feature be available.

9. I can search for a word or words anywhere in a subject heading (for example, I do a subject search for 'Angioplasty' and get records with subject headings Angioplasty, Angioplasty - Balloon, Balloon Angioplasty, etc.)

Crucial   Nice to Have   Don't Care/No Opinion   Would NOT Want
   2   1   0   -1

10. I can search for an exact subject and get a list of subjects that begin with the words I entered (for example, I can search for 'Angioplasty' and get a list of subject headings that includes Angioplasty and Angioplasty - Balloon but not Balloon Angioplasty)

Crucial   Nice to Have   Don't Care/No Opinion   Would NOT Want
   2   1   0   -1

11. When you search for subjects, do you prefer to see a list of records immediately? Or do you prefer to see an alphabetic list of subject headings such as:
Angioplasty [49 titles]

Angioplasty - Balloon [16 titles]
Angioplasty - Emergency [12 titles]
Etc.
from which you select a subject and then see records?

- Would usually prefer to see a list of records immediately
- Would usually prefer to see an alphabetic list of subject headings, select a subject, and then see the record or records with that subject heading
- Have no strong preference

Search Combinations: For each feature, please tell us how important it is to you that this feature be available.

12. I can combine author, title, subject and other searches together, in the same search (for example, I enter 'austen pride' and get a list of titles including Jane Austen's <u>Pride and Prejudice</u>)

Crucial	Nice to Have	Don't Care/No Opinion	Would NOT Want
2	1	0	-1

13. I can specify whether each term is an author, title, subject etc. (for example, I enter 'name austen' and 'title pride' and get a list of titles including Jane Austen's <u>Pride and Prejudice</u> but not Stephen Pride's <u>The Art of Austen</u>)

Crucial	Nice to Have	Don't Care/No Opinion	Would NOT Want
2	1	0	-1

14. I can combine terms, operators, and symbols in complex nested keyword searches, entered in one line (for example, I can create a search such as ((Name austen) and (Title prejudice or sense) and not (Subject biography))

Crucial	Nice to Have	Don't Care/No Opinion	Would NOT Want
2	1	0	-1

15. I can be helped in creating such complex searches with drop-down boxes, check boxes, and on-screen help

Crucial	Nice to Have	Don't Care/No Opinion	Would NOT Want
2	1	0	-1

Search Limits: For each feature, please tell us how important it is to you that this feature be available.

16. When I choose to limit a search by location, date or format, I can apply more than one limit at a time (for example, I can limit a search for Goulash to documents published in July 2003)

Crucial	Nice to Have	Don't Care/No Opinion	Would NOT Want
2	1	0	-1

17. I can search by location, date, or format alone, without entering a search term (for example, I can search for all items written in February 2003)

Crucial	Nice to Have	Don't Care/No Opinion	Would NOT Want
2	1	0	-1

Search Truncation: For each feature, please tell us how important it is to you that this feature be available.

18. When I truncate a word in a search, I can place a number after the truncation symbol to specify how many characters may follow (for example, I can enter 'assess*3' and retrieve Assess, Assesses, Assessing but not Assessment)

Crucial	Nice to Have	Don't Care/No Opinion	Would NOT Want
2	1	0	-1

19. I can truncate a word on the left as well as on the right (for example, I can enter '*generation' and retrieve both Generation and Multigenerational

Crucial	Nice to Have	Don't Care/No Opinion	Would NOT Want
2	1	0	-1

20. Are there any other Searching features that are crucial? Please specify

- _____
- _____

Navigation: For each feature, please tell us how important it is to you that this feature be available.

21. When my search returns a long list of titles, I can jump to any page within the list rather than paging through the full list one screen at a time
   Crucial   Nice to Have   Don't Care/No Opinion   Would NOT Want
     2   1   0   -1

22. When my search returns a long list of titles, I can jump to a specific record within the list rather than paging through the full list one screen at a time
   Crucial   Nice to Have   Don't Care/No Opinion   Would NOT Want
     2   1   0   -1

23. From my search results, I can hot link to an electronic version of the document
   Crucial   Nice to Have   Don't Care/No Opinion   Would NOT Want
     2   1   0   -1

Personalized Searching: For each feature, please tell us how important it is to you that this feature be available.

24. I can look back at previous searches I've done within a session, edit them, and run them again
   Crucial   Nice to Have   Don't Care/No Opinion   Would NOT Want
     2   1   0   -1

25. I can save searches that I use often under my user ID, and run them whenever I log on
   Crucial   Nice to Have   Don't Care/No Opinion   Would NOT Want
     2   1   0   -1

26. I can define my preferred sort order that the system will use every time I log on
   Crucial   Nice to Have   Don't Care/No Opinion   Would NOT Want
     2   1   0   -1

Requesting Items: For each feature, please tell us how important it is to you that this feature be available.

27. When an item is at the Library, I can request that it be pulled for me
   Crucial   Nice to Have   Don't Care/No Opinion   Would NOT Want
     2   1   0   -1

28. I can specify where I want to pick up the item that is pulled for me or where it is to be delivered
Crucial   Nice to Have   Don't Care/No Opinion   Would NOT Want
2   1   0   -1

29. I can mark multiple volumes of a title in a single request
Crucial   Nice to Have   Don't Care/No Opinion   Would NOT Want
2   1   0   -1

Imaging:

30. How important do you think electronic imaging of documents is to the Library initiate?
Crucial   Nice to Have   Don't Care/No Opinion   Would NOT Want
2   1   0   -1

Are there any other features we haven't asked about that are crucial for you? Please specify.

- _____
Crucial   Nice to Have   Not Important to me
5   4   3   2   1   0

- _____
Crucial   Nice to Have   Not Important to me
5   4   3   2   1   0

- _____
Crucial   Nice to Have   Not Important to me
5   4   3   2   1   0

- _____
Crucial   Nice to Have   Not Important to me
5   4   3   2   1   0

- _____
Crucial   Nice to Have   Not Important to me
5   4   3   2   1   0

Have you ever used a library system that you think would work for OUR? If so, please tell us about it.

_____
_____
_____

Do you have any additional comments or thoughts regarding our new Library?

_____
_____
_____

Thank you for helping us plan for the new Library!

OUR Company employees ranked this function:	Crucial 5	Nice 4	to 3	Have 2	Not 1	Importa 0
Searching by words in titles, authors, subjects, etc	15	10				
Combination searches such as combining author and title	12	10	3	1		1
Searching titles, authors, and subjects by exact beginning	9	7	5	3		2
Searching by document report number	10	5	5	1	4	2
Ability to limit searches by location, date, and format	7	6	4	3	6	1
Ability to re-sort search results	5	7	10	3	2	
Saving searches for download, email, print	15	5	4	1	2	
Email notices for document requests, recalls, etc	6	8	7		6	
Hot links within the record to electronic versions of the title	7	13	6		1	

Are there any other basic functions that you think are crucial?

Storage of paper documents and ability to "hand search".
Easy to locate the documentations.
Version control.
Literature searches on specified topics on a monthly basis.
Security of key documents.
Ability to search without complete information (ie, author's complete name)

Access and knowledge of where materials are located

Data base of all company contracts - search by company name, individual name, expiration date, etc.
Document control features locked

Each section of the survey was mapped out in an Excel spreadsheet, (shown above are the responses in the "searching function" section), so it was easy to see, by counting the total responses, what was important to the company employees. As shown, being able to search by titles, authors, subjects, document numbers and being able to save and download their search results headed the list. So these became the "MUST HAVE" requirements in searching for any software system we considered.

All comments about each section were also listed in that area so they would be in one place for review.

Yes, many people told me they were overwhelmed by the survey and did not understand why I wanted to know so much detail on their views of searching, navigation and imaging. I said I wanted to find out how experienced everyone was with library systems. It also gave me valuable information on how people viewed the function the library was going to perform.

These are some specific comments from the user survey. Very interesting.

Are there other deficiencies? Please specify.

I think the above captures it well - I prefer to work with electronic documents whenever possible and would like them to be current, available, easy to locate, and indexed logically - I prefer shared drive or SharePoint to email, because what if you're not on the right distribution list? - please note that SharePoint has a nice display but does not back up well and is not easy to restore from backup, you can ask the IT guys for more detail-

20. Are there any other Searching features that are crucial? Please specify

* I'm not clear on whether indexing of full text within the documents in the archive was assumed or not. If I'm looking for a file containing text that reads "Differences in Post-PCI Management, Depending on Periprocedural Anticoagulants" I'd like to search for an exact character string (probably just a part of the foregoing) to find the electronic file. In this case I'm not interested in all documents containing the words "Post-PCI," and "Periprocedural." I'm looking for documents containing an exact string of characters (e.g., "Depending on Peri").
* I would also like the ability to search for "Post-PCI" AND "Periprocedural" and find documents containing those two words in the body of the document (not just in the title or in meta-tags that were assigned to the document).

Are there any other features we haven't asked about that are crucial for you? Please specify.

* Document control/version control/final document stays as an electronic record of what has been submitted to a governmental agency.

* At the same time, be able to retrieve those documents and to alter them for another purpose

Have you ever used a library system that you think would work for OUR? If so, please tell us about it.

I was an Admin at Exxon Biomedical Research where they had a massive library where they had a full staff of librarians and clerks who could fulfill search requests for you or show you how to do it. All incoming and outgoing documents for the entire company were coded and classified by a certain document type and assigned a specific category number. The information in this library was not only used by Exxon affiliates but was also shared with neighboring university libraries.

Have you ever used a library system that you think would work for OUR? If so, please tell us about it.

Will all electronic materials (articles, study reports, etc.) be housed on SharePoint?
If so, need a better way to search for the articles and documents.

Do you have any additional comments or thoughts regarding our new Library?

The survey starts out great. You introduced this as document control system, which would be a structure for creating, updating, validating, and archiving of electronic files in a coherent taxonomy. And the list of deficiencies with the present system is very good. But then we lost our way in all the discussion of search engine features. The cure for our deficiencies isn't a search engine. The cure involves following a lot of document control rules that make extra work for everybody. It's like we're counting our chickens -- all those wonderful chickens that we'll be able to retrieve with the push of a button -- while forgetting the drudgery involved (for EVERYBODY in the company) in raising them.

Do you have any additional comments or thoughts regarding our new Library?

For many regulatory questions-- you just have to go in there and skim through documents till you find what you want- so we will still definitely need a fully accessible file room where one can go and look see- otherwise I am sure folk will just keep their own personal copies of the critical documents

Do you have any additional comments or thoughts regarding our new Library?

Confusion concerning the purpose of the "library". I was under the impression that the primary function was to be document storage and retrieval with security for company documents. The additional functions of a circulating library would be nice but secondary. Many documents currently in the company should be gathered together in a secure area and available when needed, i.e. clinical case report forms, reports, study documents, regulatory files, manufacturing records, computer software, etc. Most of the questions included in this questionnaire are more directed toward the function of a more traditional circulating library system and away from the idea of a document storage function.

Do you have any additional comments or thoughts regarding our new Library?

It would be nice to have a data base of all company contracts (consulting agreements, clinical site agreements, speaker agreements, etc.) in one place.

Hi Dale

My only concern with a central system is ease of access to documents for the foreign offices. For your information it takes quite some time to open documents on the Homebase public directory, although I am not aware this is the case for documents on the Intranet.

Dale:

Am a bit too green to "OUR" to provide meaningful feedback. Let me say, however, that the notion of a library is a fantastic one. The ability to search on competitors (many sources for this), probe new areas / indications (Decision Resources Database), track publications, and track pipelines (R&D Focus, etc.) have been historically very helpful to me in BD and Marketing positions. Are these being considered? If not, I'd be happy to chat about sources and information.

Chapter 5 - Review Known Software Systems

You will need to get the Information Technology (IT) department to buy-in to your plan and process very early because they are extremely important for a seamless, trouble-less installation. You want to make sure any system you select fits in well with what IT is currently operating and their plans for the future.

Ask IT:
 - what hardware and software they currently use;
 - what they like (are they Macintosh or Microsoft based or something else?);
 - the storage requirements your plan might need and will extra storage be available if required;
 - demands and needs of any new software program, i.e. how must it interact with current hardware and software systems;
 - how supportive they can be with hardware and software, will they be able to do database administration, will you have to do it or will it be done by outside providers?;
 - will they consider open source software?;
 - what department will pay for the purchase and maintenance of any software and hardware required, IT or your department?:

I found by talking with the Vice-President of IT, that Our Company was a Microsoft Windows environment, using Dell computers and SQL servers. They were not interested in UNIX, or open source software, or any system in which our data resided on another company's servers and we accessed it over the Web. This talk was very helpful in determining the software and hardware limitations the vendors had to meet. It dropped several vendors out of consideration because they did not provide us with open access to our data. They wanted to store our data on their servers. Where is the value in that? What happens when there are connection problems? We lose access to our data and can't do any work. If the data is stored in-house, we can almost always access it.

Talking to IT helped me formulate the questions that were important to them – what language is the system written in, hardware that it runs on, usage of proprietary databases or open databases, requirements of client access, pricing, support, implementation/training, etc.

Finding out IT's operations, in a way, was disappointing because I had found an open source software product which would had met all our requirements.

You should also start, if you have not already, researching software systems and software vendors thru professional associations, WWW searches, listservs, etc. Do the ones you know of meet the needs you have? Ask other professionals what they use and are aware off, how long have they used that system, how happy they are with the vendor, etc.

Doing this will give you a general knowledge of systems and may weed some out because they lack a specific function you know you need. Most companies do not put enough in-depth product information on their websites. Even having an on-line demo rarely helps because most of them focus on the features the vendor thinks are important and does not allow you to select which features you want demonstrated.

Lots of systems talk about the ease of importing records in MARC format. All our records and documents would never have any MARC formatting and so this feature was useless to us. This is a good example of something a vendor thinks is important which may not be of interest to you. Evaluate whether the system has the functionality you need to get your job done.

I did not ask any vendors for information at this time. I was content with finding information on their website, finding reviews of software systems and asking other professionals. I knew, from previous experience, I would be flooded with requests for meetings so the vendors could demonstrate their products. I did not want to waste my time and theirs viewing products which did not fit our needs.

You need to focus on a system that will work well for your needs, be compatible with other systems in house, and be useful for others in the company, rather than getting the best system money can buy.

Start by defining your needs in your terms. Think about the functions you want the system to perform and ignore the features it has. No one is more of an expert in your business than you are. You know the best way to do things, you need a system to work that way and not have to change your process to fit the system. When you look at a system demo, tell the salesman about your processes and have him show you the system doing it that exact same way.

Chapter 6 - Create Functional Requirements List

Now combine and total the scores from the survey and info audit results to show the high demand requirements. This is what the company employees think and may not be, in your view, the absolute highest requirement. The comments will add a lot of info and weight for your search.

Here is the first functional requirements list I created.

Functional Requirements - the functions in **bold** are considered must have functions

Classification and cataloging functions: does your software provide cataloging and classification functions for the materials placed in your system?

Number of possible fields: how many fields are possible?

Field size limitations? Are their limitations on the number of characters we may place into any field and if so, how many?

Notes field - free text and searchable: is there a field where we can place notes? Is this field searchable?

Indexing - field and full-text: can your system automatically index documents by full-text and by field?

Unlimited size text box or boxes: is there a field in the cataloging function where we may place a large amount of text, such as an abstract of a document?

Materials circulation function (check-in & check-out): does your system have the ability to track documents placed into circulation or loaned to an individual?

Retention management & scheduling function: we need records retention function. Does your system provide one?

Restricted user access to certain materials: does your system allow us to restrict access to certain documents or materials for a specific individual or a group of users?

Document version tracking: can your system track versions of a document as it is drafted and undergoes revisions and changes?

Transaction history - who looked at an item: can your system track what documents a user looks at and when?

Volume number field (volume number X of Y volumes): does your system have a field so we may enter volume numbers? Such as volume 1 of 14, 2 of 14, 3 of 14, and so on?

Labeling functions available - barcode, color, other: can your system print labels, and if so, what information can we put on the labels?

Possible concurrent users or viewers: how many individuals can use your system at one time? Is there a maximum number with the initial installation and will we have to buy licenses for more users?

Fields for Dewey, LC, MeSH headings: is there a field where Dewey Decimal system numbers, or Library of Congress cataloging numbers may be placed?

Degree of customization we can do - main screen, forms, etc.: how much can we customize the system and can I do it in house without help from your software support team? (i.e. No extra cost?)

Document types defined - paper, binder, folder, elec., email, etc.: what sort of document types can be defined in the system?

Media types defined - CD-ROM, video, audio, PDF, slides, etc.: we may have various types of media in the future. Is there a field for showing this?

Full text search capabilities: when we image a document, can we do full-text searching within the document?

Boolean searching capabilities: can we do Boolean searching using functions such as 'AND', 'OR', 'NOT' and so on?

Keyword search capabilities: does your system allow keyword searching?

Wildcard searching capabilities: does your system allow searching with wildcards? (Example: if I search for comput?, I get all variations such as computer, computing, computation, and so on.)

Numeric searching capabilities: does your system allow searching for numbers?

Date searching capabilities: does your system allow searching for specific dates, or within a range of dates?

Thesaurus or taxonomy building capability: does your system use a thesaurus for cataloging or does it allow for the creation of one?

Document & records management function: does your system have a document and records management function, allowing for the tracking of a document through its lifecycle?

Periodicals & serials management function: does your system have a periodicals management function, tracking the receipt, loaning and retention of periodicals?

Save desktop files and email as records: can we save files from our desktop into your system as documents? Can we import emails and save them as documents?

Output functions available- text, HTML, PDF, Word, etc.: how can we export information from your system?

Import functions available - text, PDF, Word, email, databases, spreadsheets, etc.: what types of information may we import into your system?

Ease of importing and exporting: how easy is it to import and export documents and information?

Data import routine: how do we import data? Manually, electronically, scanning or imaging?

User created defined selection reports: does your system allow us to create custom reports?

Image management capability: does your system have image management capabilities?

Document image scanning (save as OCR or text, both or either): in what format can we save images, .tiff or PDF or what?

Automated form data capture: can your system automatically capture data from fields on a form and import it into a Word or Excel document?

Web (intranet) publishing: can we use your system to create a Web page for use on our intranet?

CD-ROM publishing capabilities: can we publish documents onto a CD-ROM using your system?

Is your system compatible with Microsoft SharePoint?

Development tools and languages used: what computer languages are used to create your system?

Database format used; need an industry standard: what computer languages are used to create your database?

Software reside on server or client workstation: does your software reside on a server, or does it need to be loaded on every workstation that wants to use it?

Direct access to the data? can we direct access to our data from outside your system software?

Software specifications: what software runs your system and what do we need to run it?

Hardware required for single user and for networking: what hardware is needed to run your system?

Cost of product: what is the cost of your product?

Annual support agreement costs: what does it cost for annual support?

Annual maintenance costs: what does it cost for annual maintenance?

Optional modules for workflow, revision, auto routing: do we need to purchase optional modules to get these functions or do they come with the basic software package?

Chapter 7 - Draft Screen Layouts

Using the functional requirements list, as suggested by OUR Company employees, I started putting my thoughts into screen layout images. This helps a lot in discussions because you can point to a feature and show how it might work in that area and interact with the other areas.

When you draw screen layouts you get a very good idea what each function such as searching, circulation, data entry, administration, etc. will have to contain. This also shows what data types will appear in all functions. For example, the unique identification number will have to appear on every screen so you have to think about the best possible way to have it displayed. You know it will appear as a field by itself in the cataloging, data entry screens, and circulation screens but on a search results screen it might appear in a table form with all the other search results.

The screen shots will also show everyone what fields will show on each screen, what function must be linked to other functions; what fields should have pull-down menus and all the other features you need.

You may want to pass your draft layouts of screens and functional lists to users who expressed a lot of interest during the audits and survey and ask for their thoughts. By explaining what the Library's needs and wants are, you will find out what they think is important.

The more detailed you are in fleshing out what functions are needed to support your business requirements the better. First it will show others in your company exactly what you need and want done and removes their ability to say any old software system will do.

Second, it removes the vendors ability to say "yea, we can do that.." only to find out when you get into the evaluation process that 1) they don't do what you said, 2) they don't do what you wanted done to your satisfactions, or 3) they do part, but not all of what you need/want done, etc.

Cataloging Screen and Full Record Screen

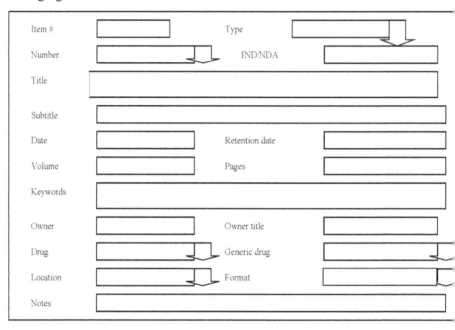

Item number is automatically generated by the system.

These fields need at least 225 characters to fit into them: Title, Subtitle, Keywords, and Notes.

Drug and generic drug field need to be tied to each other. Type in one and the corresponding value appears in the other.

These are pull down menu fields: Type, Number, Drug, Generic Drug, Location, and Format. (Shown by down arrows.)

Fields should be auto-complete. If what the Librarian types matches an existing value in that field, it should pull it up.

Librarian should be able to search from this screen but it is not mandatory.

This will also be the information shown when the full record of an item is pulled up. Without the pull down arrows.

Records Screen

Item #	Module #	Title	Volume	Date	IND/NDA
1111	2.1	CTD Table of Contents	1 of 7	10104	35287
1112	2.2	CTD Introduction	2 of 7	10104	35287
1113	2.3	Quality Overall Summary	3 of 7	10104	35287
1114	2.4	Nonclinical Overview	4 of 7	10104	35287
	2.5	Clinical Overview	5 of 7	10104	35287

5 of 15 items found	Next Screen	New Search

Clicking on any record will bring up the complete information on that record.

Like Microsoft Word or Excel, the screen should have sliding bars on the side and bottom to move you through the listings.

Clicking on Column Headings will sort by that heading.

Search Screen

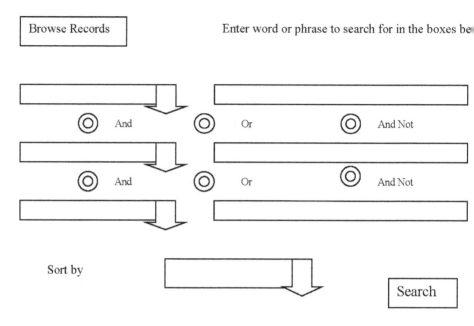

Browse Records   Enter word or phrase to search for in the boxes be|

○ And   ○ Or   ○ And Not

○ And   ○ Or   ○ And Not

Sort by   Search

Search screen should allow patrons to browse through the records so it will
need a 'Browse' button.

Left hand boxes have pull down menus to allow patrons to select what field
or fields they wish to search in. Fields may be "Anywhere", "Title",
"Number", "Keyword", "Drug", "IND/NDA", and so on.

Bottom field will allow patrons to select how they want the records sorted.
By Title, Number, Date, Drug, etc.

Patron Maintenance

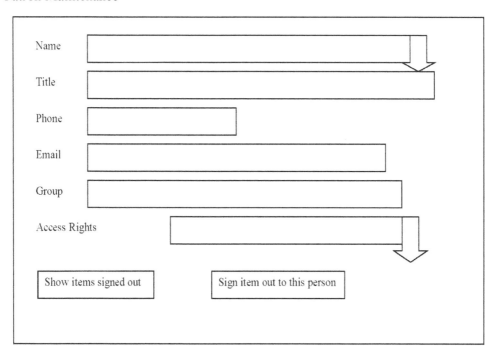

Pulling up and clicking on a name in the 'Name' field should automatically fill in the phone, email, title and group fields.

Access will be limited to several types of documents. The default will be "Regulatory", and other types may be "HR", Finance", "Legal", "Contracts".

The system will automatically refuse to sign out an item to a patron if they do not have access to that type of document.

Chapter 8 - Create Steering Committee

You should review the needs analysis you have done with various process owners, high volume users and IT. By reviewing the compiled needs with them, you may catch any omissions and also practice expressing those needs which will come in useful when speaking with vendors.

I set up a steering committee, following the suggestion of my manager, to give interested individuals the change to contribute to the process of software selection. This also removed any chance of them saying, at a later date, they had no input into the process and so remove much of their power to criticize what software system was selected. My personal feelings were educating these people about the operations of libraries would be a waste of my time. Those who supported the Library supported it, those who saw me and the Library as a threat to their powerbase opposed me and tried to derail the process and those who did not care one way or the other basically ignored it all.

VPs, Directors and Managers from these groups were invited to participate in the Steering Committee. As long as we had one person from each group, I was happy.

Senior VP responsible for the whole Product Infrastructure group
Regulatory
Safety
HR
Accounting and Finance
Legal
Manufacturing
Medical Writing
IT/IS
Clinical Data
Investor Relations
Biostatistics

I also set up small focus groups to provide input on parts of the requirements. In the focus groups, I could set up a laptop and LCD projector, go through a demo on a vendor's websites and get immediate feedback on what the users thought about the software. It gave me concrete knowledge about the look and feel the users were interested in. Most of them preferred a document management system which resembled the Windows Explorer layout over other layouts. I believe it is a learning curve issue, the users now find Windows Explorer so comfortable they choose it over other layouts, even if the other layout is better.

I selected, with the help of my manager, one or two individuals from all the departments within the company. I asked them to participate and let them decide if only one or both would attend the meetings. This provided input from all over the company and allowed for various viewpoints to be presented.

This is the email I sent to process owners to invite them to become part of the steering committee:

Hello All,

I am inviting you to join a steering committee that will provide input on the purchase of a document management system.

Why you?
1. because you are involved in one of the major processes within OUR,
2. because you may require access to the regulatory documents kept within the Library,
3. because you provided valuable information on how the Library can best serve OUR,
4. because you are an important customer of the Library.

In this charter meeting, we will discuss why we are looking at document management systems and the value one would provide to OUR.

Your contribution will be to:
1. make sure I am not missing any important data on how information moves within OUR,
2. confirm the role and use of the regulatory documents which are the main focus of the Library,
3. help me clarify the requirements for a user-friendly interface to the document management system.

Thank you,
Dale Carpenter

At the first meeting I discussed the benefits of going digital by using the "Let's Go Digital" presentation and the return on investment by using a document management system, "Library ROI and Document Management". Before the meeting I sent everyone a copy of the presentations with this email:

Attached are the slides I will be using at this afternoon's meeting to explain why we are meeting, the Group's scope, and the contributions the Group may make.

'Library ROI and doc management' – details what OUR process owners said would be the best function the Library could perform for them, has an introduction to 'document management', and the tasks of the Steering Group.

We may not go into details of document management systems but if we do, I thought you should have the following in case the issues are brought up.

'Let's go digital' - has justification for introduction of the imaging component of a document management system.

'Software matrix' - compares several document management systems I have looked at which have met over 90% of the functions I believe are important.

'Software matrix definitions' - explains each function.

If you have any questions or any personal experience with document management systems, please let me know.

The "Let's Go Digital" presentation:

1. Got Digital?
2. many arguments for paper
   - portable
   - more convenient
   - legal admissibility

74

- read without special equipment or a technology learning curve
3. paper
   - takes up a lot of space
   - cannot be searched by content
   - cannot be transferred physically down multiple pathways without large cost & effort
4. Modern documents not just paper – electronic media includes letters, invoices, proposals, documents, engineering drawings, emails, Word files, spreadsheets, databases, HTML web pages, etc.
5. all of these
   hard to organize
   difficult to find and share
   very difficult to keep under control
6. value of information on paper lies in its reuse, not its storage measure how many times a document is used, not how much room it takes up
7. several benefits of going digital - beyond saving space or trees:
   ease of making copies of the digital records
   simple costs savings with elimination of print and copying costs
   multiple users and access levels are possible
   ease of information dissemination and low shipping costs
8. use of digital records in vital records and disaster recovery plans
   - no loss of quality from generation to generation with digital images
   - digital easier to store/manage/access than paper – provided files are precisely indexed and ordered
   - - digital content searchable allowing documents to be quickly and accurately searched and located
   - - better operational/process efficiencies – communication and distribution of documents across the enterprise
9. Disadvantages include:
   Not human-readable without computer equipment
   Significant equipment costs possible, including hardware and software
   Potential for hardware and software obsolescence

Indexing requirements may be more extensive than is required with other formats

Digital quality control and metadata capture and management are complex and time consuming processes requiring expertise and constant vigilance

10. digital provides more than tidier offices or improved filing systems

empowers all areas of the business to use information more effectively to drive revenues and profitability

improvements in changed business processes are the real benefits

difficulty in cost-justifying digital document management

no analysis and measurement of operational parameters before investing

almost impossible to quantify success afterwards

counting filing cabinets is not the answer

11. How do we assign dollar figures to these benefits?

Productivity improvements?

Support enterprise-wide improvement activities?

Promote common templates/metrics across the company?

Major reductions in cycle time: document creation/revision/signoff?

12. What is ROI of these?

How can we determine that?

13. Linking a document management system and an imaging system gives the ability to gain these benefits:

Faster delivery of document to user's desks

Improved awareness and availability of document data

Provide business management, project management, and financial management groups with improved access to supporting documents

14. **How much does it cost a company for employees to look for information?**

Lewis, Mobilio & Associates (Jan 2001) says 1.8 hours per day (108 minutes) which is 22.3% of their time

Delphi Group (2010) says 73% of employees surveyed said they spent 4 or more hours a week which is +20% of their time

15. Rough estimate

Average annual salary = $100,000*

Divide by 250 workdays per year = 400

Divide by 480 minutes per day (A) = $0.83
Time spent looking for files (B) = 10 minutes
Multiply A x B for $ / day / user lost =$8.30
Multiply by 250 days for $ lost / year / user = $2,075
Multiply by 200 OUR employees = $415,000
*Global HR Director 9/7/2010

16. Other benefits ($):
- paper cost savings
- copier equipment maintenance cost avoidance
- telephone cost savings
- postage/shipping cost savings
- staff payroll savings (who copies documents & how many?)

17. **Less Quantifiable (Soft) Benefits**
Improved quality - productivity enhancement from using correct, up-to-date files (reduced errors)
Faster time to market - productivity enhancement from faster reviews and approvals
Improved innovation - productivity enhancement from sharing information
Sustainable competitive advantage - increased efficiency and effectiveness of employees
Improved decision making - immediate access to information
Improved communication - automated electronic distribution of documents

18. Costs
- Server hardware
- Server software
- Network hardware (routers, etc.)
- Network software
- Additional hardware (scanners, storage, PCs, upgrades, etc.)
- Additional software (licenses, viewers, etc.)
- Related maintenance fees on hardware and software
- Software licenses
- Related Software maintenance & support
- System related salaries
- IT staff technical training (fee + opportunity costs)
- User training (fee + opportunity costs)
- Clerk (initial load setting up / importing)
- Services (Installation, setup, deployment)
- Other

19. paperless office is as useful as paperless toilet
    we want to allow fluid movement of information
    between paper and digital worlds
20. Thank You
21. Dale Carpenter

The "Library ROI and Document Management" presentation:

1. **Librarian**
   OUR Company
   Date Posted: 06/06/10
   Salary: Open
   Type: Full Time – Experienced
   Ensure that documents are stored and retrieved in accordance to regulatory requirements.
   Additional tasks and projects as needed.
2. **What Library function or functions would provide the greatest return to you and your department?**
   Question asked during Information Audits with OUR Process Owners
3. To **archive, manage and retrieve** documents ('track only versions of the official document') for OUR in a secure and controlled location, while making an inventory of the documents available to all employees of OUR.
   IT Director
4. Making **access** to the paper documents retained in the library as painless as possible. Person 1
5. Keeping GMP and compliance documents in a secure location **easily accessible** in the event of   an FDA visit.
   Manufacturing Person
6. Controlled **access** to employee records.
   Human Resources Person
7. **Storing** department documents in a secure area, and having them **organized** in a logical, easy to understand manner so I may find them right away when I need them.
   Clinical Person
8. Secure retention of documents including security layering so department personnel can quickly and easily obtain needed documents when required but no one else may **access** the regulatory documents.
   Regulatory Person

78

9. Create guidelines for corporate wide folder and file **naming protocols** to enable easier access to and retrieval of information.

    Corporate Person

10. Having a person who **knows where things are** to cut down the hassle of finding items. Drug Safety Person

11. **Storage and access control** (both here and off-site) of finance and legal documents such as tax returns, vendor payable files and the employee expense reports with receipts would be a valuable function of the Library.

    Finance Person

12. An **integrated data warehouse** would be very useful as a repository for all data from a project or trial. This would ensure all data, no matter what format it was in, could be located and accessed when needed.

    Clinical Person

13. For due diligence requests, a "**virtual data room**" holding the documents which are usually requested would be a time and money saver.

    Finance and Legal Persons

14. A **document classification** system easily understood by everyone in the organization. Person 1

15. Having the drug development data we obtain from the licensing company accessible **in electronic form** for use by company departments such as Regulatory and Publications. Business Development Person

16. A company policy or system for **document naming and filing**, so everyone would know how to name and where to file documents. This would greatly speed document retrieval. Clinical Person 2

17. **Control and storage of documents** during the trials. Clinical Person 3

18. Having as many documents as possible available and accessible in **an electronic format.**

    Person 1

19. Primary function of Library

    SECURE CONTROL OF,
    EASY ACCESS TO,
    QUICK RETRIVAL OF
    REGULATORY DOCUMENTS

20. Secondary functions of Library

    Electronic access to documents and data
    Document classification system / naming protocols

21. A document management system can do these functions
> We could build one in house
> but why re-invent the wheel?

22. What is
> document management?
> Document management is the system of controlling both paper-based and electronic information from its creation to its archival or destruction.

23. Content Sections of Document Management (DM)
> Create
> Collect
> Distribute
> Manage
> Archive
> Verify/secure
> Retrieve/search

24. Management Sections of DM
> Plan/Manage
> Integrate
> Operate
> Train
> Outsource

25. DM Includes
> Library Functions
> Workflow Management
> Retrieval and Viewing
> Access and Security
> Document Importation and Storage (Imaging)

26. Library Functions
> Cataloging and classification
> Indexing – field, full-text and keyword
> Inventory
> Records retention
> Search functions by various means
> Check-in and check-out
> Report creation

27. Workflow Management
> Create, share, review, publish and organize documents
> Manage document revisions
> Manage access to documents
> Track transactions (who looked at what)
> Manage and control document templates
> Keep workgroups informed of changes

28. Retrieval and Viewing
>Retrieve and view documents or images by title, author, date, number, keyword, etc.
>Control level of access – none, read-only, read & write, copy, print
>Audit trail of users

29. Access and Security
>Control levels of access to system, directory, groups of documents, document, down to page or paragraph level
>Access may be controlled at group or individual level by group manager
>Track and audit users

30. Document Import and Storage
>Storage of document in many formats – Word, Access, Excel, PowerPoint, Adobe Acrobat, HTML, text, photographs, etc.
>Conversion of documents from one format to another while retaining the original
>Full-text index each document as it is saved
>OCR form capture

31. First We Focus On
>Library Functions
>Retrieval and Viewing
>Access and Security
>To control the paper regulatory documents
>These functions will answer your needs as expressed in Info Audits

32. Second focus
>Generalize functions of document management system to include non-regulated documents

33. Scope of Steering Group
>Represent Regulatory requirements to make sure Library meets them
>Provide information on previous experiences with document management systems
>Clarify requirements for user-friendly interface

34. Steering Group Tasks
>Provide any personal knowledge of or experience with document management systems to me by a certain date

35. Thank You
Dale Carpenter

After the meeting, I sent out the meeting minutes:

-----Original Message--

From: Dale Carpenter
Sent: Date and Time
Subject: Steering Group August 10 Meeting Minutes

Document Management Software Steering Group Meeting

Dale Carpenter called this meeting to discuss the need for a document management system within OUR. Such a system would "ensure that documents are stored and retrieved in accordance to regulatory requirements", one of the tasks which he was hired to perform.

Dale introduced himself and mentioned he had performed Information Audits with primary process owners in June 2010. One of the questions asked during the audits was "What Library function or functions would provide the greatest return to you and your department?" The primary function requested was to provide 'secure control of, easy access to, and quick retrieval of regulatory documents'. Secondary functions were 'electronic access to documents and data' and 'companywide document classification system and naming protocols'.

A discussion of document management (DM) functions led Ed to say that we should beware of scope creep and that one of the next steps should be to define the scope of the DM project; what is to be done by when and what the budget of the project should be.

After discussion, it was agreed the scope would focus only on the control of the paper regulatory documents after they are published.

Moe brought up the point that he, Larry, and Curly were concerned with the regulations of the SEC and the rest of the company was concerned with abiding by the FDA regulations. So we really have multiple 'buckets' of regulatory documents to be concerned with.

It was suggested a subgroup be formed that will examine the actual needs a DM system should fulfill.
Abe, Bobby, Charlene, Darlene, Ed, Frank, Garn and Dale volunteered to be members of the group.

The subgroup will take on these action items:
1. Define scope of project - what needs to be done by when

2. Revisit 'needs' vs. 'nice to have' functions of library/document management software.

I sent the entire Steering Committee, the "Necessary functions of OUR Library" document, with screen shots, in which I had drawn up the functions a software system needed to have, based on my audits and surveys. Of course, some people wanted to put their noses into a section of the system they would not be working with and had no knowledge of. So I gently reminded them I was the expert in this area and would be dealing with those details.

From: Dale Carpenter
Sent: Date and Time
To:
Subject: RE: Search Functions of Software

Hello All,

I asked you to concern yourselves ONLY with the 'Search' function because that is the only part of a Library software system you will be interacting with, you need to be comfortable with it, and I would like to know if I am overlooking any important aspects of it.

We will look at software systems after this group "2. Revisit 'needs' vs. 'nice to have' functions of library/document management software." which is what we agreed to in the September 23 meeting.

Again, please focus only on the 'needs' and the 'nice to have' of the Search function and let me know if I am overlooking anything.

Thank you,
Dale

The next meeting had these issues resolved:

From: Dale Carpenter
Sent: Date and Time
Subject: August 12 Meeting Minutes

The group discussed the functions necessary for searching in a library document management system. They were:

Full-text across all fields;
Boolean searching capabilities: using functions such as 'AND', 'OR', 'NOT';
Keyword;
Wildcard (Example: search for comput* will find variations such as computer, computing, computation, etc.);
Numeric;
Date;

Number of concurrent users - This was felt to be a very important issue because access to the documents must not be limited to only a certain number of individuals at one time.

A 'browse' function is needed for patrons who just want to browse through the records.

'Basic' and 'Advanced' search screens may not be needed if enough searching capability is provided on a 'Basic' screen.

We need the ability to sort results by title, date, drug, module number, etc.

'Help' button leading to search tips for the patrons.

Can patron email a request for an item to the Librarian through the system? This was felt to be a requirement.

Other capabilities discussed were:

A unique identifier is needed for each item and it would probably be the FDA number because OUR employees refer to documents by using it.

All fields should be alphanumeric.

Searching should not be case sensitive.

The ability to search by phrases is required.

Search results must be limited by the access level of the searcher. If the searcher does not have access to a certain class of documents, they should not see those documents listed at all.

Discussing these functions logically brought up the question of how documents would be distributed or made available to users. This could be by providing paper copies or by access to images of the documents. Dale will draft the first version of the issues involved, and the group will meet again to discuss this.

So I created this document and sent it to the Steering Committee:

Distribution of documents from OUR Library

To ensure that controlled documents are stored and retrieved in accordance to various requirements, the process of allowing access to the controlled documents must be discussed. These assumptions have been made. What else, according to your requirements, needs to be discussed?

Basic Assumptions:

The original controlled document will be kept in the Library and should not leave the Library.

Access to documents will be allowed only to those with a need to know the information in that specific document and sufficient authorization from the department head of the group that created the document.

The department head of the group which created the document must provide, in writing, a list of who will be allowed to have access to the document. This list should be by title, or functional group within OUR.

OUR employees will require access to documents quickly, and from various OUR locations. The options for providing access are:

1. Have library staff available 24 hours a day, 7 days a week to provide access to documents in the Library.
2. Duplicate all documents at all OUR locations.
3. Duplicate some of the documents at all OUR locations.
4. Use a document imaging system to provide access to documents from all OUR locations.

Option 1 would require the hiring of 3 or more staff members for the Library.

Options 2 and 3 would require copies of the documents (plainly marked as copies) to be created, logged as copies in the Library management system, and assigned to the other OUR sites that require them. To ensure safekeeping of OUR confidential and sensitive information, a specific person at each site will be responsible for the control, tracking and management of the copies.

Options 2 and 3 would require, as newer versions of the documents are placed in the Library, copies to be made and sent to the other sites to replace the older versions. The older versions would have to be destroyed as per company policy relating to the documents.

Options 2 and 3 would require each copy to be marked with the OUR location where it is stored so if the information becomes public, the source of the information leak would be known and action could be taken to make sure information leakage does not happen again in the same manner.

With Options 3 and 4, documents would be copied or imaged as they are requested. Not all documents would need to be copied or imaged.

Options 2 and 3 will require physical space at each OUR location to store the copies. Option 4 would eliminate the need for physical storage space.

Assumptions and issues relating to paper documents:

If an OUR employee requires a paper copy of a document, it will be created, checked out to them and tracked in the Library management system.

If a paper copy of a document is created, it would be printed on colored paper to graphically show it was not an original document. Other methods, such as printing "copy" or another mark or date on each page could also be used to plainly show that item is a copy.

If an employee desires a paper copy of a document, how long should the employee be allowed to keep the document?

If an employee needs only a part of a document, should that be recorded and tracked? If so, how?

Employees need to be reminded of the need to control OUR information and documents and to destroy them when they are no longer needed and not to throw them into wastebaskets. How does the Librarian ensure the paper copy of a document is returned to the Library or is destroyed in accordance with OUR policy?

Assumptions relating to document imaging system:

The Library management system must provide a link from a document record to an image of that document, if the document has been imaged, to allow for easy and quick access.

The Library management system should allow a user to request a document through electronic means, if the document has not been imaged.

The document imaging system must protect access to documents through various levels of security, allowing users to see only the files they are authorized to view.

The document imaging system should track all user activities for audit purposes.

The document images should be 'read only'.

Imaged or scanned documents should never be assumed to be the same as the original paper document.

When should an employee get a paper copy, instead of using the imaged document? And who decides this?

Having the VP of IT as a manager helped immensely when it came to planning the project. We set out our goals, risks, budget, staff, schedule and procedures for the purchase of a records/document management system. This let everyone know the project's scope which defined in detail what we would do. It also defined what we would not do. "After discussion, it was agreed the scope would focus only on the control of the paper regulatory documents after they are published." That statement was developed in a steering committee meeting and evolved into this scope statement which was sent to all vendors.

> The business requirements are:
> 1. Archive, manage & retrieve paper regulatory documents for OUR in a secure and controlled location.
> 2. Provide an inventory of the library holdings searchable by all OUR employees.
> 3. Control access to the paper regulatory documents based upon the OUR employee's roles.
> 4. Track all usage of the paper regulatory documents with audit trails.
>
> In the future, we will add document imaging, workflow management, and other library functions but right now we are focusing only on the specific requirements listed above.

Whenever any end user or vendor wanted to talk about other features, I would just point to the scope statement and tell them this was all we were interested in right now.

Chapter 9 - Draft Policies and Standard Operating Procedures

Once the major decisions about how documents were to be handled were agreed upon, I drafted up policies and operating procedures for the Library. It is best to do them first as a flowchart, with precise step by step instructions as to what will happen, and then put those steps into a written format. You can see how the following flowcharts will easily transform into an operating procedure.

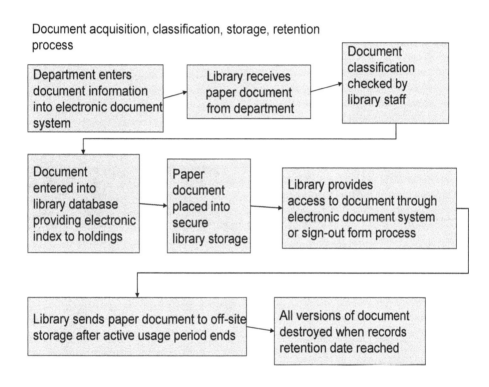

Document acquisition, classification, storage, retention process

Department enters document information into electronic document system → Library receives paper document from department → Document classification checked by library staff

Document entered into library database providing electronic index to holdings → Paper document placed into secure library storage → Library provides access to document through electronic document system or sign-out form process

Library sends paper document to off-site storage after active usage period ends → All versions of document destroyed when records retention date reached

Access to Library documents process

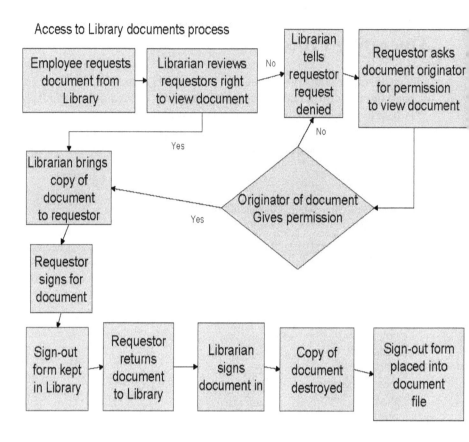

Employee requests document from Library → Librarian reviews requestors right to view document

No → Librarian tells requestor request denied → Requestor asks document originator for permission to view document

Yes → Librarian brings copy of document to requestor

No → Originator of document Gives permission

Yes → Librarian brings copy of document to requestor

Librarian brings copy of document to requestor → Requestor signs for document → Sign-out form kept in Library → Requestor returns document to Library → Librarian signs document in → Copy of document destroyed → Sign-out form placed into document file

Chapter 10 - View Vendor Sites with Functional Requirements in Hand

Next I wrote the needs analysis and requirements into questions requiring a 'yes' or 'no' answer, so I could easily see if the vendor's existing system met OUR needs right out of the box or would require some modifications. This Requirements Document is shown in Chapter 11 in the form I sent to vendors.

Having this Requirements Document in hand, I reviewed software systems from 51 different vendors. A lot were eliminated because I could easily see that their structure did not meet our requirements. Many of them were quickly eliminated because they did not have any tracking functions that our company needed to meet regulatory requirements. Many others, while having the ability to give each item a unique identification number, did not have any label printing ability included. Still others that focused on electronic document management had no means to catalog, index and track paper documents which would never be made into an electronic format. We have one document with 618 volumes. Imagine sitting down at a paper scanner and turning it into electronic files? (I scanned it two years after the software was installed in order to allow electronic access to it.)

Again, focus on the functionality of each system and not the features. Does the system have the functions you need to do your job? Remember that demonstrations show the best capabilities and features of the system, not its limitations. And ask if all of the features shown are available off-the-shelf or are they add on custom features which cost extra?

Don't let the system cost be your only guide because installation and training are significant factors in how quickly you can get the system up and running to return value to your company.

Chapter 11 - Requirements Sent to Vendors

I could now email vendors about my search for software. I briefly told them I was looking for a software system for the company Library, I had quite specific needs and those needs were listed in the Requirements Document. If they were interested, please fill out it out and return it to me. I gave them a deadline of one month. This is the email message I sent to 15 selected vendors.

I have been hired by Our Company (OUR), a fast growing pharmaceutical firm, to create a secure library for our paper regulatory documents. I am now investigating software systems that will meet the business requirements of the library.

The business requirements are:
1. Archive, manage & retrieve paper regulatory documents for OUR in a secure and controlled location.
2. Provide an inventory of the library holdings searchable by all OUR employees.
3. Control access to the paper regulatory documents based upon the OUR employee's roles.
4. Track all usage of the paper regulatory documents with audit trails.

In the future, we will add document imaging, workflow management, and other library functions but right now we are focusing only on the specific requirements listed above.

Will you please let me know if your product can fulfill our requirements by answering the questions in the attached document?

I drafted screen images to help envision the requirements and functions and have included them with the questions. These are drafts and your screens do not have to look anything like these, as long as your system meets all of our requirements.

Thank you.

This is the Requirements Document I created and sent along with the above email.

Functional operations of OUR Library:

Please answer each question yes or no. We are interested in an out-of-the-box solution but if your system can meet our requirements with very little customization, please tell us. Thank you.

Search Screen

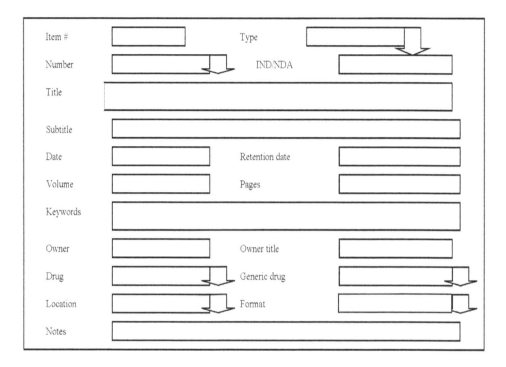

Search screen should allow patrons to browse through the records so it will need a 'Browse' button.

Left hand boxes have pull down menus to allow patrons to select what field or fields they wish to search in. Fields may be "Anywhere", "Title", "Number", "Keyword", "Drug", "IND/NDA", and so on.

Bottom field will allow patrons to select how they want the records sorted. By Title, Number, Date, Drug, etc.

Search capabilities

We want these search capabilities for both the Librarian and the patrons. Can your system provide them?
Full-text across all fields;
Boolean searching capabilities: using functions such as 'AND', 'OR', 'NOT';
Keyword;
Wildcard (Example: search for comput* will find variations such as computer, computing, computation, etc.);
Numeric;
Date;

How many individuals can use your system at the same time? Is there a maximum number with the initial installation and will we have to buy licenses for more patrons?

System should have a 'browse' function for patrons who just want to browse through the records. Does your system provide this?

We do not need 'Basic' and 'Advanced' search screens. One search screen is enough if it gives multiple boxes for entry of search terms and search functions. Patrons must have three or four fields in which they can enter search words or phrases, with Boolean logic selector buttons (and, or, and not) and pull down fields to show what fields they want those words or phrases searched in. Does your system provide this?

Patrons should have the ability to sort their results by title, date, drug, module number, etc. Does your system provide this?

Is there a 'Help' button leading to search tips for the patrons? Can the Librarian edit the help tips?

Can patrons save their searches?

Can patrons export their search results?

Librarian must be able to search items by status, such as checked in/out, label printed yes/no. Does your system provide this?

Can a patron email a request for an item to the Librarian through your system?

Cataloging Screen and Full Record Screen

Item #	Module #	Title	Volume	Date	IND/NDA
1111	2.1	CTD Table of Contents	1 of 7	10104	35287
1112	2.2	CTD Introduction	2 of 7	10104	35287
1113	2.3	Quality Overall Summary	3 of 7	10104	35287
1114	2.4	Nonclinical Overview	4 of 7	10104	35287
	2.5	Clinical Overview	5 of 7	10104	35287

5 of 15 items found	Next Screen	New Search

Item number is automatically generated by the system.

These fields need at least 225 characters to fit into them: Title, Subtitle, Keywords, and Notes.

Drug and generic drug field need to be tied to each other. Type in one and the corresponding value appears in the other.

These are pull down menu fields: Type, Number, Drug, Generic Drug, Location, and Format.

Fields should be auto-complete. If what the Librarian types matches an existing value in that field, it should pull it up.

Librarian should be able to search from this screen but it is not mandatory.

This will also be the information shown when the full record of an item is pulled up. But it will not have the pull down arrows.

Classification and cataloging functions:

How many records can your system handle?

There must be a field which automatically gives each new item cataloged into the database its own unique number. This will be used for inventory control and printed on the barcode. Does your system provide this?

How many fields are possible on the cataloging screen? We need at least 17. How easy will it be for me to modify this screen to add more fields or customize field size or attributes?

Are there limits on the number of characters we may place into any field and if so, how many? We need several fields (title, subtitle, keywords, and notes) with a minimum of 225 characters.

Is there a field in the cataloging function where we may place a large amount of text (minimum 225 characters), such as an abstract of or notes about the document and have it full-text searchable?

Is there a field for defining types (paper, binder, folder, elec., email, CD-ROM, video, audio, PDF, slides, etc. or can we customize one for this? It must be drop down form field.

We have multiple volumes in a module. How easy is it to create or copy duplicate records where the only difference is the number of the volume? (vol. 1 of 14; vol. 2 of 14; etc.)

We will have an original item and copies of that item. How does your system show this?

A retention management & scheduling function field is needed to tell when item is to be destroyed. Does your system have such a field?

We will have one field showing the generic name of a drug and another showing our market name for that drug. These two fields should be locked so when typing one value, the other will automatically be filled in. Does your system provide this?

We will have one field showing the module number of a document and another showing the module title. These two fields should be locked so when typing one value, the other will automatically be filled in. Does your system provide this?

Several fields must be drop down form fields for ease of cataloging. Example: number field (module numbers); drug and generic drug; location; format. Does your system provide this?

Fields should be auto-complete sensitive. Does your system provide this?

Can your system create parent/child relationships, to show files within a box?

Can I search from the cataloging field?

Can I perform batch updating of files? How easy is it?

Is data entry based on user-defined rules?

Can I import data from other systems like Access, Excel and Word? Or export data to other systems like Access, Excel and Word?

Label and Print management

System must be able to print labels with item number, barcode, color strip for filing and inventory functions. Does your system have a barcode labeling and printing function built in? Or do you sell or recommend 3rd party software?

System must allow for inventory being done by barcode. Hand held barcode reader scans shelves and items on shelves, then when placed in docking cradle, downloads inventory into system. System generates report showing what is on shelves, what is missing, what is signed out and what is miss-filed on wrong shelf. Does your system provide this?

What printer or printers do you require or recommend for your system?

Does your system require us to buy custom labels from you?

Does your system have the ability to queue printing requests to use a full label sheet?

Records Screen

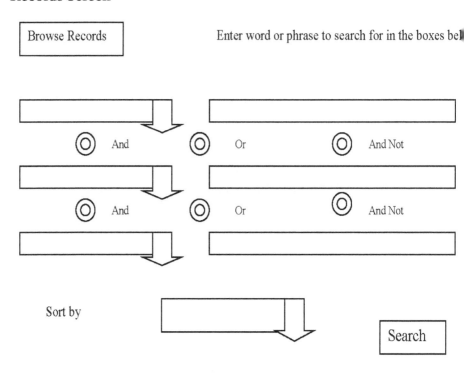

Browse Records

Enter word or phrase to search for in the boxes be[

And   Or   And Not

And   Or   And Not

Sort by

Search

Clicking on any record will bring up the complete information on that record.

Like Microsoft Word or Excel, the screen should have sliding bars on the side and bottom to move you through the listings.

Clicking on Column Headings will sort by that heading.

Record viewing screen:

Records should be displayed with fields such as module number, title, date, system number, etc. in columns. Clicking on any column heading will sort by that heading. Using scrolls bars will let viewers move left or right to view other columns and up and down to see all records. Does your system provide this?

How many records show on screen as default? Does your system tell how many records were in the search results? Does it show search terms used?

Clicking on any record should bring up the full information about that record. That screen will have 'Back to list', 'Previous', 'Next', and 'New Search' buttons to aid in viewing records. It will also have a 'Request Item' button so the patron can let the Librarian know they wish to borrow that item. Does your system provide this?

Patron Maintenance Screen

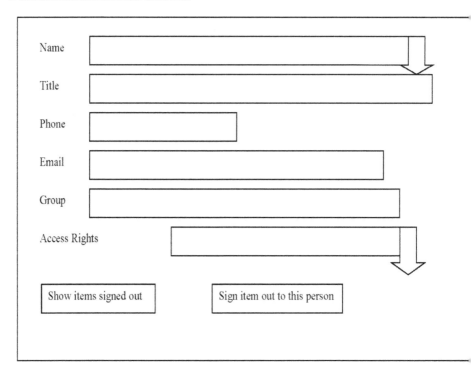

Pulling up and clicking on a name in the 'Name' field should automatically fill in the phone, email, title and group fields.

Access will be limited to several types of documents. The default will be "Regulatory", and other types may be "HR", "Finance", "Legal", "Contracts".

The system will automatically refuse to sign out an item to a patron if they do not have access to that type of document.

Materials circulation function (check-in & check-out):

Librarian will be the only one with check-in and check-out rights. Can your system provide this?

Patron Maintenance module must include ability to restrict patron loan access to certain materials and track transaction history. Does your system provide this?

On circulation screen and patron maintenance screens, the 'name', 'phone', and 'email' fields should be linked so pulling up a name will automatically fill the other fields. Does your system provide this?

We will limit access to documents. This field should be a drop down form field with 4 or 5 values. "Regulatory" will be the default value unless another is chosen. The system must refuse to sign out documents if the patron does not have access rights to that type of document. Does your system provide this?

Pulling up a patron record must automatically show what they have signed out and when it is due. Does your system provide this?

The circulation module must provide a weekly overdue report showing what is overdue and who has it. Librarian should have ability to set what day of week report will be run and also to run it at any time. Does your system provide this?

What are the default sign out periods? Can the Librarian change them?

System must retain and be able to show full transaction history on every event for every record for our audit purposes. Does your system provide this?

Report management:

Librarian must have to ability to generate reports using multiple criteria and to select the order the fields appear in. Does your system provide this?

Inventory reports will be generated by barcode scanning of shelves and items and also by criteria selected by Librarian. Does your system provide this?

Can we create custom reports such as transaction history of items checked out and in; records listed by owner, retention date, or any other criteria?

How many pre-configured reports come with your system?

How can we export data from your system?

Can we save user defined reports so we can quickly run them again?

We have multiple locations. Can your system generate reports showing the unique items at each location and what items are at two or more locations? Can your system show originals and copies and where each are located?

Please answer these questions in detail. Thank you.

Does your system have an easy to use Windows interface?

Degree of customization we can do - main screen, forms, reports, etc.: How much can we customize the system and can I do it in house without help from your software support team?

Software specifications: what software runs your system and what do we need to run it?

Hardware required for single patron and for networking: what hardware is needed to run your system?

Development tools and languages: what computer languages are used to create your system?

Database format; is it an industry standard: what computer languages are used to create your database?

Software resides on server or client workstation: does your software reside on a server, or does it need to be loaded on every workstation that wants to use it?

Does your system support a WAN (wide area network)?

Do we have direct access to our data from outside your system software?

Cost of product: what is the cost of your product?

Annual support agreement costs: what does it cost for annual support?

Annual maintenance costs: what does it cost for annual maintenance?

Is training included or does training cost extra? How is training done, in-house, on-line, or at your company?

Is there on-line help and is this included in the cost of the system? What are their hours?

Who uses your software? Please give me references I can talk with who have been using your software for over 1 year and for over 5 years.

How long will it take to implement the software on our system?

How big is your company, how many years have you been in business, how many years have you been selling and supporting this specific software?

When is the next revision of the software due? Is it a minor or major revision? How many revisions has the software gone through? When was the last one?

Does the technology rely upon 3rd party software or hardware? And if so, how long have you had this relationship and how strong is the relationship? Provide names at the other company(s) I can talk to.

Vendors will tell you they can do everything you need. Tell them you will see no demonstration until they completely fill out the Requirements documents. Firmly let them know you can only compare software systems by having them answer the questions set out in your Requirements Documents and this is the only way you can compare apples to apples. If the company does not fill out the document, they are not considered. No exceptions.

Vendors will try to sweet talk you. Ask them to imagine they are buying a new car. Ask them if they would waste their time test driving a car which obviously could not meet their needs. If they would not waste their time, why should you waste your time looking at a system which does not meet your needs? Promise to email or call them to let them know if they are one of the vendors that you select to further research.

Some vendors will call to ask you what are your must have items, your nice to have items and what questions are just information gathering questions. Tell them you need all questions answered to judge their system, so in effect, everything is a must have function.

These salespeople will pressure you for a meeting; ask to show you a demo, and pressure you to look at their system. Just keep telling them this is the first step in how you are evaluating software systems and if they do not want to answer the questions, you will be glad to drop them from consideration. Don't back down.

Many times I had to explain that since OUR Company was a very unique case and not a traditional library, a traditional library system would not work. We needed document tracking and not many systems will show you the entire history of a document's use. We needed to restrict access to certain documents and most systems do not have that ability. I got very good at explaining this to vendors.

Send more emails to vendors setting out your process. Some vendors won't reply right away. I received the first replies from some vendors 2 months after I emailed their websites. Guess they weren't very interested in new business.

If a vendor sends you the Requirements Document with blank or vague answers, return it and ask them for specific information. Tell the sales representative to send the questions to a technical rep with your contact information. Remind them a blank or vague answer will get them dropped out of consideration.

This will go on for several rounds with certain vendors. The sales people will tell you the technical people will answer all your questions after you see a demo, or they can modify their system to do anything you need it to do, including making coffee for you in the morning. Just keep telling them this is the first step in how you are evaluating software systems and if they do not want to answer the questions, you will be glad to drop them from consideration.

Several vendors told me this was the most exacting and precise information request they had ever received from a company. I took that as a complement.

Chapter 12 - Create Value Weighting Spreadsheet to Compare Systems

To compare the software programs side-by-side, I created an Excel spreadsheet with our requirements in the left column. A vendor's name was put in the top of a column and their answers entered in the row corresponding with the question.

Send an email asking for specific answers if you see blank or vague answers. Ask for the stock numbers of any items they want you to purchase, such as labels, binders, printers, etc. Grab the supply catalog your office manager uses for ordering supplies and check to make sure these are generic products and not a custom item you must purchase from the vendor.

I requested information from 15 vendors. 8 vendors filled out our Requirements Document. The other companies either did not reply or said their systems would require too many modifications to cost-effectively meet our requirements.

Add value weighting to the sections of the Excel spreadsheet deemed most important to your needs and user's needs. Decide what functional requirements are most important (searching, data entry, circulation, administration, etc.). Score each yes answer from a vendor in that section with a certain number of points, a modification needed with fewer points, and no function available earns negative points. For all other sections, a yes gets so many points, modification needed gets fewer, and no function earns zero points. Enter a formula at the bottom of each function area and at the bottom of the spreadsheet to total the points.

Here is the formula that puts values in for the YES, NO and MOD answers.

   =IF(B10–"YES",3,IF(B10="Mod",1,IF(B10="NO",-1)))

Put this formula in the column to the right of the column where you enter the company's answer. In the example below, Company One's answers are put in the "B" column so the formula is put into the "C" column. If YES is entered into cell B10, a 3 is entered into cell C10. The formula selects the word value placed in the cell to its left.

The Excel formula used to total all the "YES" answers at the bottom of the spreadsheet for the 'B' column was:

=COUNTIF(B1:B176,"YES")

Or you could just total all the sums in column C by using:

=SUM(C10:C219)

Comparing vendors this way you can see how they compare in each functional area and how they compare overall.

Oh, if you think this is complicated, try to imagine the spreadsheet with 8 companies.

TOTAL POSSIBLE IF ALL OPERATIONS WERE MET	152		152		152	
TOTAL OF FUNCTIONAL OPERATIONS MET	Company 1 **115**		Company 2 **126**		Company 3 **136**	

VENDORS ABILITY TO MEET REQUIRED LIBRARY MANAGEMENT FUNCTIONS **USER FUNCTIONS**	Company 1		Company 2		Company 3	
SEARCH CAPABILITIES:						
Can your system provide search capabilities for both the Librarian and the patrons:						
Full-text across all fields;	YES	3	YES	3	YES	3
Boolean searching capabilities: using functions such as 'AND', 'OR', 'NOT';	YES	3	YES	3	YES	3
Keyword;	YES	3	YES	3	YES	3
Wildcard;	YES	3	YES	3	YES	3
Numeric;	YES	3	YES	3	YES	3
Date;	YES	3	YES	3	YES	3
How many individuals can use your system at the same time?	LICENSING		SEVERAL THOUSANDS		LICENSING	
Is there a maximum number with the initial installation and will we have to buy licenses for more patrons?	LICENSING		3. NEED MORE LICENSES		5. NEED MORE LICENSES	
Does your system have a 'browse' function for patrons who just want to browse through the records?	YES	3	YES	3	YES	3
One search screen with three or four fields for search words or phrases, with Boolean logic selector buttons (and, or, and not) and pull down fields to show where those words or phrases searched. Does your system provide this?	YES	3	YES	3	YES	3
Patrons should have the ability to sort their results by title, date, drug, module number, etc. Does your system provide this?	YES	3	YES	3	YES	3
Is there a 'Help' button leading to search tips for the patrons?	YES	3	YES	3	YES	3
Can the Librarian edit the help tips?	YES	3	NO	-1	YES	3
	Company 1		Company 2		Company 3	
Can patrons save their searches?	NO	-1	YES	3	YES	3
Can patrons export their search results?	YES	3	YES	3	YES	3
Can Librarian search items by status, such as checked in/out, label printed yes/no?	YES	3	YES	3	YES	3
Can a patron email a request for an item to the Librarian through your system?	YES	3	MOD	1	YES	3
RANKING FOR SEARCH CAPABILITIES FUNCTIONS:	41		39		45	

LIBRARY FUNCTIONS
CLASSIFICATION AND CATALOGING FUNCTIONS

109

Question	Company 1		Company 2		Company 3
How many records can your system handle?	UNLIMITED		UNLIMITED		UNLIMITED
There must be a field which automatically gives each new item cataloged its own unique number. This will be used for inventory control and printed on the barcode. Does your system provide this?	YES	3	YES	3	YES
How many fields are possible on the cataloging screen? We need at least 17.	20		32		20
Is it easy for me to modify this screen to add more fields or customize field size or attributes?	NO	-1	YES	3	YES
We need several fields (title, subtitle, keywords, notes) with a minimum of 225 characters. Can your system provide this?	YES	3	YES	3	YES
Is there a field in the cataloging function where we may place a large amount of text (minimum 225 characters), such as an abstract of or notes about the document and have it full-text searchable?	YES	3	YES	3	YES
Is there a field for defining types (paper, binder, folder, elec., email, CD-ROM, video, audio, PDF, slides, etc or can we customize one for this? It must be drop down form field.	YES	3	MOD	1	YES
	Company 1		Company 2		Company 3
We have multiple volumes in a module. Is it easy to create or copy duplicate records where the only difference is the number of the volume? (vol. 1 of 14; vol. 2 of 14; etc.)	YES	3	YES	3	MOD
We will have an original item and copies of that item. Will your system show this?	YES	3	MOD	1	YES
A retention management & scheduling function field is needed to tell when item is to be destroyed. Does your system have such a field?	YES	3	YES	3	YES
We will have one field showing the generic name of a drug and another showing our market name for that drug. These two fields should be locked so when typing one value, the other will automatically be filled in. Does your system provide this?	MOD	1	YES	3	YES
We will have one field showing the module number of a document and another showing the module title. These two fields should be locked so when typing one value, the other will automatically be filled in. Does your system provide this?	YES	3	YES	3	YES
Does your system provide drop down form fields for ease of cataloging? Example: module number field; drug and generic drug; location; format.	YES	3	YES	3	YES
Fields should be auto-complete sensitive. Does your system provide this?	YES	3	YES	3	YES

Question	Company 1		Company 2		Company 3	
Can your system create parent/child relationships, to show files within a box?	YES	3	YES	3	YES	3
Can I search from the cataloging field?	YES	3	YES	3	YES	3
Can I perform batch updating of files?	NO	-1	YES	3	YES	3
Is data entry based on user-defined rules?	YES	3	YES	3	YES	3
Can I import data from other systems like Access, Excel and Word?	YES	3	YES	3	YES	3
Can I export data to other systems like Access, Excel and Word?	YES	3	YES	3	YES	3
RANKING FOR CLASSIFICATION AND CATALOGING FUNCTIONS:	44		50		52	

	Company 1		Company 2		Company 3	
LABELING AND PRINTING FUNCTIONS:						
System must be able to print labels with item number, barcode, color strip for filing and inventory functions. Does your system have a barcode labeling and printing function?	YES	3	MOD	1	YES	3
System must allow for inventory being done by barcode. Does your system provide this?	MOD	1	MOD	1	YES	3
What printer or printers do you require or recommend for your system?	ANY WINDOWS STANDARD		ANY WINDOWS STANDARD		ANY WINDOWS STANDARD	
Can we use labels from any supplier with your system?	YES	3	YES	3	YES	3
Does your system have the ability to queue printing requests to use a full label sheet?	YES	3	NO	-1	YES	3
RANKING FOR LABELING AND PRINTING FUNCTIONS:	10		4		12	

	Company 1		Company 2		Company 3	
PATRON MAINTENANCE & MATERIALS CIRCULATION:						
The Librarians will be the only one with check-in and check-out rights. Can your system provide this?	MOD	0	YES	1	YES	1
Does your Patron Maintenance module include ability to restrict patron loan access to certain materials and track transaction history?	YES	1	YES	1	YES	1
On circulation and patron maintenance screens, some fields should be linked so pulling up a name will automatically fill the other fields. Does your system provide this?	YES	1	YES	1	YES	1
We will limit access to documents. Does your system provide this?	YES	1	YES	1	YES	1
The system must refuse to show documents if the patron does not have access rights to that type of document.	YES	1	YES	1	YES	1

111

	Company 1		Company 2		Company 3
Pulling up a patron record must automatically show what they have signed out and when it is due. Does your system provide this?	MOD	0	YES	1	YES

| | Company 1 | | Company 2 | | Company 3 |

	Company 1		Company 2		Company 3
Does circulation module provide weekly overdue report showing who has overdue items? Librarian should have ability to set what day of week report will be run and also to run it at any time.	YES	1	YES	1	YES
Can the Librarian change the default sign out periods?	MOD	0	YES	1	YES
Does your system retain and show full transaction history on every event for every record for our audit purposes?	YES	1	YES	1	YES
RANKING FOR PATRON MAINTENANCE & MATERIALS CIRCULATION FUNCTIONS:	6		9		9

REPORT FUNCTIONS:

	Company 1		Company 2		Company 3
Librarian must have to ability to generate reports using multiple criteria and to select the order the fields appear in. Does your system provide this?	YES	1	YES	1	YES
Inventory reports will be generated by barcode scanning of shelves and items and also by criteria selected by Librarian. Does your system provide this?	YES	1	MOD	0	YES
Can we create custom reports such as transaction history of items checked out and in; records listed by owner, retention date, or any other criteria?	YES	1	YES	1	YES
How many pre-configured reports come with your system?	180		5		20
Can we save user defined reports so we can run them again?	YES	1	YES	1	YES
Can your system generate reports showing the unique items at each location and what items are at two or more locations?	YES	1	YES	1	YES
Can your system show originals and copies and where each are located?	YES	1	YES	1	YES
RANKING FOR REPORT FUNCTIONS:	6		5		6

	Company 1		Company 2		Company 3
RECORD VIEWING SCREENS:					
Does your system display records with fields such as module number, title, date, system number, etc in columns? Clicking on any column heading will sort by that heading.	YES	1	YES	1	YES
Using scrolls bars will let viewers move left or right to view other columns and up and down to see all records.	YES	1	YES	1	YES

112

How many records show on screen as default?	ALL		26		ALL	
Does your system tell how many records were in the search results?	YES	1	YES	1	YES	1
Does it show search terms used?	NO	-1	YES	1	NO	-1
Does clicking on any record bring up the full information about that record? That screen will have 'Back to list', 'Previous', 'Next', and 'New Search' buttons to aid in viewing records.	YES	1	YES	1	YES	1
'Request Item' button so the patron can let the Librarian know they wish to borrow that item.	YES	1	MOD	0	YES	1
RANKING FOR RECORD VIEWING FUNCTIONS:	4		5		4	
SYSTEM HARDWARE AND SOFTWARE						
Does your system have an easy to use Windows interface?	YES	1	YES	1	YES	1
Can I customize the system in house without help from your software support team?	NO	-1	YES	1	YES	1
What software runs your system and what do we need to run it?	IIS, SQL SERVER		SQL SERVER		SQL SERVER	
What hardware is needed to run your system?	PROVIDED		WINDOWS 2000		PROVIDED	
What computer languages are used to create your system?	GUPTA & HTML		C++		VISUAL BASIC	
What computer languages are used to create your database?	SQL SERVER Company 1		SQL SERVER Company 2		SQL SERVER Company 3	
Does your software reside on a server, or does it need to be loaded on every workstation that wants to use it?	SERVER		WORKSTATION OR WEB BROWSER		WORKSTATION	
Does your system support a WAN (wide area network)?	YES	1	YES	1	YES	1
Do we have direct access to our data from outside your system software?	YES	1	YES	1	YES	1
Is your user and security applications integrated with Windows Active Directory?	NO	-1	YES	1	YES	1
Is it a function of your software to log out users after a period of no activity?	NO	-1	YES	1	NO	-1
Is training for administrator, IT staff, and users included or does training cost extra?	INCLUDED		INCLUDED		INCLUDED	
Is training done in-house, on-line, or at your company?	ON-SITE		ON-SITE		ON-SITE	
Is there on-line help and is this included in the cost of the system? What are their hours?	8-8 EST		9-5 EST		8-5 EST	

113

Who uses your software? Please give me references I can talk with who have been using your software for over 1 year and for over 5 years.	PROVIDED	INCLUDED	PROVIDED
How long will it take to implement the software on our system?	6-8 WEEKS	3 WEEKS	4 WEEKS
How big is your company, how many years have you been in business, how many years have you been selling and supporting this specific software?	10 YEARS, SELLING 10 YEARS	15 YEARS, SELLING 4 YEARS	100 YEARS, SELLING 10 YEARS
When is the next revision of the software due? Is it a minor or major revision? How many revisions has the software gone through? When was the last one?	YEARLY	4Q 2004 MAJOR REV, LAST MINOR 4Q 2003	2 MAJOR REVS APRIL & OCTOBER
RANKING FOR HARDWARE AND SOFTWARE	0	6	4

	Company 1		Company 2		Company 3	
Additional Capabilities for Future Consideration						
Integrated Electronic Document/Image Management	YES	3	YES	3	YES	3
Zone OCR	NO	-1	YES	3	NO	-1
FDA, HIPAA or other agency compliant	NO	-1	NO	-1	NO	-1
Document Workflow	YES	3	YES	3	YES	3
RANKING FOR ADDITIONAL CAPABILITIES	4		8		4	
TOTAL POSSIBLE IF ALL OPERATIONS WERE MET	152		152		152	

	Company 1	Company 2	Company 3
TOTAL OF FUNCTIONAL OPERATIONS MET	115	126	136

114

Chapter 13 - View System Demonstrations

Invite the highest-ranking vendors in for demonstrations of their products, having them show the specific functions you need. "I need a system to do this. Please show me your system doing this specific function." Tell them to ignore everything else until the end of the demo.

Make it very plain to the vendors you do not care at all about the extra bells and whistles their system may have. You want and need to see the basic functions. After all of your questions on the basics are answered, then you will look at everything else.

Make sure you go over every point on your requirements list. Don't let them give you a guided demonstration, add your own records in and play with them. One vendor's product looked very nice until I noticed their system did not auto-complete typing in a field. When you will be entering thousands of records into a system, auto-complete typing is a nice function to have.

Another software system said on the functional requirements list we could easily customize any screen. So I asked the vendor to add another field to a screen. He did not know how to do it and said something about how their support people would do all the customizing we needed. I ended that meeting politely right then.

Explain how your processes work and how you do something and ask the salesman to show the system doing it that specific way. You don't want to change your process to fit the system, the system needs to fit your process.

You can have users and process owners attend for another set of eyes but that may distract you from specific functions. However, those users can provide feedback on how easy they think the system is to use, which is important. Since we needed an imaging function and not many individuals in the company understood what it was, I invited the Steering Committee members to sit in on a demonstration of one imaging system. It was much easier talking about that function after the demo.

It is difficult to hold vendor demonstrations because you are trying to explore and examine a system, have your questions answered, and take notes about the product. I found it useful to have their Requirements Document with me and have a recording device to capture all of the conversation, which I used to complete my notes after the meeting.

Ask the salesmen for references and also search for some on your own. Ask the references these questions and any others you can think of:

> How long have you used the system?
> How many people use the system? What is their background?
> How much training was provided? Was it on-site, by phone or computer?
> What other systems were used previously?
> How often do mistakes make it into the system? What kind of mistakes?
> How much tweaking did your other systems need before this system was completely compatible?
> How helpful is the vendor's phone support and how thorough is the training?

You want to find a company with strong commitment to customer support and a record of ongoing product improvement. Find out about the local representative or support office and visit it if you can. This might give you some good insights as to their capabilities and personality.

Chapter 14 - Send Vendors Request for Proposal

Invite those vendors who meet your requirements and who are interested to submit a proposal to you. This request for proposal should include such things as the number of users; the number of sites; the type of software and hardware the system will be functioning on; and so forth. The vendors should have most of this information by this time from all the conversations they have had with you.

The proposals must be submitted as detailed line item proposal. Do not accept a proposal with one total figure because everything must be broken out into its components. This includes software, hardware needed, labor, installation cost and time estimates, training cost and time estimates, yearly maintenance, etc. This lets your manger know precisely what will show up in his budget and what might be an expense for another department such as IT.

This is the email I sent requesting a line item proposal.

Dear Vendor

In preparing the capital expense request for submission next week, I would like the most detailed financial figures possible. This will show management exactly what will be purchased at what cost and our Information Technology department exactly what hardware and software will be utilized and needs to be purchased. Providing such detail greatly speeds our approval process.

Would you please write your pricing proposal in detailed line item format to include all hardware and software needed to operate your system? Assume we are starting from scratch and tell us what specific hardware and software we would need for your system, basing the needs on these assumptions:
 - Microsoft based computer system using SQL Server
 - one department, one administrator entering data, with 50 concurrent users accessing the system
 - 100,000 records
 - users accessing the system through company intranet, not WWW based.
 - labels (include color coded indexing, barcode and text) printed with desktop PC and color printer
 - hand held bar code reader .

We will expand the system next year into document imaging and workflow management, used by other departments, but to get the system in house I am presenting it as a document management system for the Library.

If you have any questions please give me a call. Thank you.

I also sent the vendors this list of questions about the installation and configuration of the software and the training they will provide. You want to prevent "project creep" in which a vendor says a part of their project will take a certain amount of time, and when it takes longer for some reason they want to charge you more money. Question every part of the project in detail so you know what to expect when something does not go as expected. And of course, something will. Remember Murphy's Law.

As the system installation/configuration/training period is critical to Our Company (OUR) and your company, we need to clarify some questions so there will be fewer misunderstandings during that time.

1a. Does the installation and configuration take place at the same time or does configuration take place after installation?
1b. Does your quote express this time in hours or days?
1c. If the installation or configuration take less time than you expect, will the price quoted be reduced?
1d. If the installation or configuration takes more time than you expect, what will we be charged and is this an hourly rate or a daily rate?
1e. What is your daily rate for on-site consulting?
1g. What preparation will our IT group have to do prior to installation?

2a. Does your quote for training include training for the administrator, the OUR IT staff who will be working with the system, and training for users?
2b. How long is the training for the administrator?
2c. How long is the training for the IT group?
2d. How long is the training for the users? It should not be more than half a day.
2e. Since we have multiple users who will not be able to attend one scheduled session, at least 2 sessions must be planned for OUR Company at this location. Does your user training quote include this?
2f. Since we have users elsewhere, we would like to have a half-day training session there. Does your quote include this?
2g. How many users do you like to have in a session?

3a. Are system manuals provided for the administrator?
3b. Are system manuals provided for the IT staff?
3c. Are help manuals or handouts provided for the users?

4. Is your user application and security application integrated with Windows Active Directory?

119

5a. Is it a function of your software, and not Microsoft Windows, to log out users after a period of no activity?
5b. How long is that no-activity period and can the administrator modify it?

6. If a user does not have access rights to view a document, does the document record show when they run a search?

You should also ask these types of questions to find out more about their level of service.

"Do you have alliances with software or hardware vendors?" They may try to steer you towards specific products. Ask for a range of products from different companies and the pros and cons of each.

"Are you doing the work (installation, training, etc.)?" Find out how many individuals will be involved, their level of experience and where they are from.

"Have you worked with any smaller companies in my industry?" They must understand the technical needs of smaller companies with smaller technical support and budgets and know the regulatory requirements, if any.

"Who is the project manager?" Make sure that person is easy to reach, can talk with you without using too much technical jargon and understands your unique needs.

"Will you support the system after it is installed?" It is best to be supported by the people who installed the system, not a third party who may not be aware of your unique functions.

"What will I learn from you?" On-site training, collaboration with the IT team, and full documentation of the system is absolutely critical.

"What don't you do well?" Be skeptical of anyone who says they can do everything.

"How much are you going to cost me?" Insist on a flat fee, payable upon them reaching certain milestones. You might pay them 25 percent up front, another portion when each goal is met and the balance upon completion.

Review all of the proposals and enter this data into the value weighted matrix to adjust the vendors ranking. You can also add in other extra functions each system has which you might be adding in the future.

At this point you may ask for a copy of the vendor's administrator manual and the user's manual, which the end user would get. How does the user's manual read? Does it read like it was written by a computer expert or by a library expert? You want a manual which reads like it was written by an end user for another end user, with no computer or library jargon. Sort of a

"Dummy's Guide" to the software system. If anyone wants to learn more, they can look at the administrator's manual or you could have a training class for those interested users.

You could have a second demo with users and process owners attending. This will give them a chance to ask questions and provide you with feedback on the look and feel of each system. Sometimes the end users ask questions which you have overlooked. A classic case of "forest for the trees" tunnel vision.

Chapter 15 - Create Capital Expense Requisition

I next put together the Capital Expense Requisition document. It explained the process for determining functional requirements, the value rating system, reference checking, and the recommended vendor. It also included the specific reasons why the other vendors were not selected. Pricing information was provided, along with the costs for any other hardware, software or supplies we would need. Since we would be moving documents from one location to another, estimated costs of the move were also included.

CAPITAL EXPENSE REQUISITION
LIBRARY DOCUMENT MANAGEMENT SOFTWARE

Summary: A list of functional requirements for the Library was created and multiple vendors were investigated for a software solution. Those who provided specific answers to our list of requirements were invited to demonstrate their products.

VENDOR #2 is recommended as the solution because it can meet all of our requirements, is easily customizable for our specific needs, and has a local representative (LOCAL REPRESENTATIVE near Homebase) to do the installation and for technical support. The total cost for this project including moving the controlled documents from Faraway Town is $122,452.

Our Company Library has these requirements for managing company controlled documents:

1. Archive, manage & retrieve paper regulatory documents for OUR in a secure and controlled location.

2. Provide an online inventory of the Library holdings searchable by all OUR employees.

3. Control access to the paper regulatory documents based upon the OUR employee's roles.

4. Track all usage of the paper regulatory documents with audit trails.

A list of functional requirements was created reflecting the needs of the OUR Library and the needs of OUR employees concerning controlled documents, after meeting for information audits with company process owners and with the Library Software steering group.

After investigating over fifty vendors of library, records and document management software, fifteen were asked if they could provide a solution which met or exceeded our needs. Eight of the fifteen companies replied to our list of Functional Requirement questions. These vendors were invited to demonstrate their products. The other companies either did not reply or said their systems would require too many modifications to cost-effectively meet our requirements.

An Excel spreadsheet of our functional requirements was created, the company responses entered and totaled. The spreadsheet and the list of functional requirements are included along with the quote information and marketing materials from the vendors who met our requirements.

Function Ranking
Since certain functions (Classification and Cataloging; Search Capabilities; Labeling and Printing; and Additional Capabilities) are deemed more important than other functions, they were given more value when ranking the vendors. If a vendor met a requirement in that function they were given a score of 3. If their system required a modification to meet the function, they were given a score of 1 and if they did not meet a requirement, 1 point was deducted.
In all other functions, meeting a requirement gathered 1 point. If not meeting the requirement a point was deducted and if a modification was required, 0 points were awarded.

The remaining vendors and product were VENDOR #3, VENDOR #1, and VENDOR #2, with rankings of 115, 126 and 136 respectively.

References were provided by all vendors and several were contacted for their opinion on the products. All were satisfied with the products and would purchase them again. The references are in the answers to our functional requirements. VENDOR #2 also provided a list by industry of companies who use their products.

Recommendation

VENDOR #2 is recommended as the solution because it can meet all of our requirements, is easily customizable for our specific needs, and has a local representative (LOCAL REPRESENTATIVE near Homebase) to do the installation and for technical support. The total cost for this project including moving the controlled documents from Faraway Town is $122,452.

From Hoovers Research Company (www.hoovers.com)
VENDOR #2
20 Elmwood Blvd
Localburg, WY 12345
Phone: 111-111-1111
Fax: 800-222-2222
http://www.VENDOR #2.com

VENDOR #2 wants to keep its customers satisfied. Accordingly, it makes a variety of products. A lot more crap about VENDOR #2 follows.

Vendors Eliminated

These vendors were eliminated because they lacked these specific functions:

VENDOR #4 had fields of only 70 characters, did not support Boolean searching, was not integrated with Windows Active Directory which would greatly simplify user administration and required us to use their custom labels.

VENDOR #5 did not support barcode labeling, records retention, and did not maintain a full audit trail of transactions.

Microsoft does not sell any library management software solutions nor do any third party vendors provide library management solutions that run in SharePoint. Therefore, SharePoint was eliminated because it lacks all application functionalities including it does not generate a unique identification number for each item, does not support any labeling or barcode inventory functions; does not maintain a full audit trail of transactions; does not allow the Librarian to generate Library usage reports; and does not allow users to request an item through the system.

VENDOR #6 did not support any barcode labeling, printing, or inventory functions; did not allow the Librarian to generate reports and did not allow users to request an item through the system.

VENDOR #7 did not allow for importing or exporting of data; did not show what users had signed out; did not allow for Boolean searching and required us to use their custom labels.

Price Quote Information
VENDOR #2's proposal came in two parts, (Phase 1) paper document management and (Phase 2) document imaging and workflow management. Both Phases were combined.

VENDOR #1 provided Intranet Based and Network Based quotes. The Network Based quote was used.

Some vendors did not provide quotes for the cost of certain items. Therefore, the middle quote of all other vendor quotes was used except for the computer workstation price ($1,334.66) which was provided by John in IT on November 17, 2010.
VENDOR #1 did not provide pricing for a computer.
VENDOR #2 did not provide pricing for a computer, color printers, or labels for printing.

The travel costs to Faraway Town to perform complete inventory of documents and oversee the packing for movement to Homebase was provided by Office Manager on November 11, 2010. Thirty five dollars a day was added for meals.

A computer workstation is needed in the Library to hold the computer, printer and barcode reader. The pricing for a workstation and a stool was taken from the 2010 Village Office Supply catalog.

The estimated costs to ship the documents from Faraway Town's file room by Fed Ex ground was provided by Office Manager on November 23, 2010.

You should now meet individually with the process owners and users who are supportive of you and the project to show them your recommendation, ask for feedback and their support in the steering committee meeting. You must build a support base before the meeting at which you present your recommendation. You want to make it an easy decision for all concerned.

Using the "Vendor Selection Process" presentation showed the steering committee exactly how I went about the process of selecting the vendor I choose, and why I chose that vendor over other vendors.

You will be the one making the decision on what system to purchase because you are the expert. But it is very helpful to gather support for your choice.

If it happens, for some reason, another system is chosen over your recommendation, don't waste your energy fighting the choice. Explain calmly your reason for thinking another system is better but assure everyone you will do your best with the company's choice. (This happened at OUR when the VP of IT chose an in-state vendor over my recommended out-of-state vendor.)

VENDOR SELECTION PROCESS

1. Librarian OUR Company
    Date Posted: 06/04/10
    Salary: Open
    Type: Full Time – Experienced
    Ensure that documents are stored and retrieved in accordance to regulatory requirements.
    Additional tasks and projects as needed.
2. Primary function of Library
    SECURE CONTROL OF, EASY ACCESS TO, AND QUICK RETRIVAL OF REGULATORY DOCUMENTS
3. Secondary functions of Library
    Electronic access to documents and data
    Document classification system / naming protocols
4. A library management system can do these functions
    We could build one in house but why re-invent the wheel?
5. Functional Requirements Created

Functional requirements for the Library management system were created from user information interviews and Steering Committee subgroup of: Mr. Regulatory, Mr. Learning, Mr. Chemist, Mr. Compliance, Ms. Clinical Trial 1, Ms. Clinical Trial 2, Mr. Info Tech

6. Functional Requirements

Search Capabilities
Classification & Cataloging
Labeling & Printing
Patron Management & Materials Circulation
Report Generation
Record Viewing Screens
System Hardware & Software

7. SEARCH CAPABILITIES

Can your system provide these search capabilities: Full-text across all fields; Boolean searching capabilities (using functions such as 'AND', 'OR', 'NOT'); Keyword; Wildcard; Numeric; Date;

How many individuals can use your system at the same time?

Does your system have a 'browse' function for patrons who just want to browse through the records?

Patrons should have the ability to sort their results by title, date, drug, module number, etc. Does your system provide this?

Can patrons export their search results?

Can a patron email a request for an item to the Librarian through your system?

8. CLASSIFICATION AND CATALOGING

There must be a field which automatically gives each new item cataloged its own unique number. This will be used for inventory control and printed on the barcode. Does your system provide this?

How many fields are possible on the cataloging screen? We need at least 17. Is it easy for me to modify this screen to add more fields or customize field size or attributes?

Is there a field where we may place a large amount of text (minimum 225 characters), such as an abstract of or notes about the document and have it full-text searchable?

We have multiple volumes in a module. Is it easy to create or copy duplicate records where the only difference is the number of the volume? (vol. 1 of 14; vol. 2 of 14; etc.)

A retention management & scheduling function field is needed to tell when item is to be destroyed. Does your system have such a field?

9. LABELING AND PRINTING

System must be able to print labels with item number, barcode, color strip for filing and inventory functions. Does your system have a barcode labeling and printing function? System must allow for inventory being done by barcode. Does your system provide this?

10. PATRON MAINTENANCE & MATERIALS CIRCULATION

Does your Patron Maintenance module include ability to restrict patron loan access to certain materials and track transaction history?

We will limit access to documents. Does your system provide this?

The system must refuse to show documents if the patron does not have access rights to that type of document.

11. SYSTEM HARDWARE AND SOFTWARE

Does your system have an easy to use Windows interface?

Can I customize the system in house without help from your software support team?

What software runs your system and what do we need to run it?

What hardware is needed to run your system?

What computer languages are used to create your system?

What computer languages are used to create your database?

Does your system support a WAN (wide area network)?

Is your user and security applications integrated with Windows Active Directory?

Is training for administrator, IT staff, and users included or does training cost extra?

Who uses your software? Please give me references I can talk with who have been using your software for over 1 year and for over 5 years. How long will it take to implement the software on our system?

How big is your company, how many years have you been in business, how many years have you been selling and supporting this specific software? When is the next revision of the software due? Is it a minor or major revision? How many revisions has the software gone through? When was the last one?

12. VENDOR SELECTION PROCESS

51 software vendors of library management software solutions were investigated

15 were asked if they could provide a solution for our needs – they were emailed a list of our functional requirements

8 of the 15 vendors replied to our list of functional requirements. (Company answers available upon request)

The other companies either did not reply or said their systems would require too many modifications to cost-effectively meet our requirements

The answers from the 8 vendors were entered into a matrix and the number of yes answers were totaled

The vendors were asked again for specifics on any question they left blank or answered no

13. These 8 companies were invited to demonstrate their products Vendor 1, Vendor 2, Vendor 3, Vendor 4, Vendor 5, Vendor 6, Vendor 7, Vendor 8

Vendors gave demonstrations either in-house or online via webex

5 of the 8 vendors were eliminated because they did not meet specific functional requirements we need

14. Since certain functions are deemed more important than other functions, they were given more value when ranking the vendors:

If function met: if function not met: if mod required

Search Capabilities	+3	-1	1
Class & Cataloging	+3	-1	1
Label & Printing	+3	-1	1
Additional Capabilities	+3	-1	1
Patron Maintenance	+1	-1	0
Report Functions	+1	-1	0
Record Viewing	+1	-1	0
Hardware & Software	+1	-1	0

15. Remaining vendors and product and their rankings were:

    Vendor 1 - 115

    Vendor 2 - 126

    Vendor 3 - 136

16. References were provided by all vendors and several were contacted for their opinion on the products. All were satisfied with the products and would purchase them again.

17. Vendor 3 is recommended as the solution because:

    It can meet all of our requirements

    It is easily customizable for our specific needs

    It has a local representative (Local Rep Incorporated in Closeby) to do the installation and for technical support

18. Companies using Vendor 3 include Grinch, Horton Corporation, Chadwick Moose, and Bartholomew Cubbins

19. Business information and several screen shots of the Vendor 3 product are inserted here.

20. Library Software Steering Committee

    January 24, 2010 – met and discussed vendor selection process

    Action items:

    Subgroup to confirm regulatory needs of Regulatory group are met in overall system requirements

    Confirm a appropriate transition plan exists for moving documents from Otherplant to Homebase

21. Subgroup of Mr. Regulatory, Mr. Chemist, Ms. Clinical Trial 1, Mr. Info Tech, and Dale Carpenter met Thursday January 27, 2010 at 2 pm

22. The regulatory needs of managing physical documents were reviewed to ensure that they are represented in the library management system requirements. The needs were expressed as "manage, inventory and archive physical regulatory documents, apply records retention functions, and

provide multi-user and multi-site access to qualified OUR employees.

23. The consensus of the group was that the functional needs of managing physical documents are represented in the library management system requirements.

24. Draft of proposed transition plan was sent to all steering committee members Thursday, January 27, 2010 3:19 PM. A separate transition plan meeting will be convened and all who express interest will be invited to attend. This meeting will be scheduled after approval of the system.

25. Recommend decision on proposed solution. The recommended vendor has said they can install their system in 4 to 6 weeks after a purchase order is signed. In order to implement the software installation, it is formally recommended the steering committee approve the selection and sign off on the purchase order.

Here is an example of a line item proposal. This shows management exactly what each part of the project will cost. Don't forget to include at least 10% of the total for any contingencies.

Library Management Software Project
Itemized Listing of Capital Expenditure Requisition Request

Software	Vendor #2 Software Base License	$55,555	
			$55,555
Hardware	Add'l library desktop computer	$1,550	
	Desktop scanners (2)	$10,000	
	Color barcode printers (2)	$1,000	
	Bar code reader/scanner (2) hand held	$1,000	
	Bar code reader/scanner desktop (1)	$800	
	2 SCSI cards and cables	$2,400	
			$16,750
Miscellaneous	Label media for bar coding (3000)	$150	
	Travel to Faraway Town to conduct inventory & oversee packaging of documents for shipment to Homebase	$1,550	
	Computer workstation and stool for Library	$500	
	Shipping documents from Faraway Town	$1,500	
	Temporary help at $25.00 per hour for 1 month to scan documents	$4,000	
			$7,700
Installation, configuration and training	Professional Consulting	$22,000	
			$22,000
Annual maintenance & support	Annual Maintenance & Support	$10,000	
			$10,000
	Sub-total		**$112,005**
	Sales Tax @ 6%		**$6,720**
	Contingency costs of 10%		**$11,873**
	Project Total		**$130,598**

133

Chapter 16- Submit Proposal to Management

Submit the recommendation to management with only 3 software providers. In your report, have a high-end product, a low-cost product, and your selection in the middle of that price range. Edit the matrix down to only those three vendors so you can show they will all do the job but your selection gives the best value for the price.

I created a binder for each high level manager who would be reviewing our purchase. In front was the Library Document Management Software article, next was the Expanded Software Matrix spreadsheet showing precisely how each of the three final products ranked against each other and next were sections on each vendor showing printouts from their websites that included company history, product lines, and contact information.

Include a description of the vendor selection process to show how you arrived at the final decision.

Support your recommendation with sound relevant reasons. You chose this company because it did everything you need it to do, it has local support, it has a very friendly user interface that give a quick learning curve for the users and it is available at a reasonable price compared to other products. And why is it better than the other two you have listed. Sell the system in meetings and get verbal agreements to purchase it.

Get the sign-off on the vendor paperwork right after the meeting. Walk all necessary paperwork around to every department that is involved. You will need the vendor to provide a tax number for your accounting department. Accounting will set up a new vendor account in their system if your company has not purchased anything from that vendor.

You will need to send the vendor a copy of the signed purchase order for them to start work on your project.

Chapter 17 - Install Software

Have a kick-off meeting with your selected vendor to set requirements, expectations, and timelines for work completion. Both the vendor representative and the technical representative who will be doing the installation should be at this meeting. You should also have your IT people there to talk with the tech rep about what will be needed and what is required.

Draft an implementation plan with timelines and get buy-in from IT. The plan should include an overview of the process; a detailed scope section with the steps of installation for each product and/or feature; what needs to be configured and how it will be configured; the roles and responsibilities of everyone involved; the steps in the installation and training; list of hardware and software and who will provide it; and a timeline for doing everything.

The tasks section should look something like this, including steps, days to perform, start and finish dates and total time. If they don't meet the timeline, ask for a discount.

Installation Date: 4/4/10
Requirements Met Date: 4/6/10
Training Date: 4/6/10
Finish Date: 4/7/10

ID Task Name	Start	Finish	Days Used	%Work Complete
1 Approve Functional Specification	3/29	3/29	0	50%
2 Approve Application Prototype/Label Design	3/29	3/29	0	50%
3 Phase I Software Installation	4/4	4/5	1	0%
4 Approve System Acceptance Test for Phase I	4/5	4/5	1	0%
5 Requirements session for Phase II (Afternoon)	4/6	4/6	1	0%
6 VENDOR #2 Training for Phase I	4/6	4/7	2	0%
7 Total Days Used on This project			5	

Have the vendor do any required customization and demonstrate the customizations so you know they can meet your functional requirements before you sign off on the system.

Most vendors will work with you to determine the characteristics and functionality you require from their system. They will write a functional specification detailing what they will do for you, when it is to be accomplished and who has certain roles and responsibilities. Read this carefully and ask a couple other people, like your IT manager, to review it. There will be a phrase somewhere stating something like "Additional functionality not specifically outlined in this document will be handled outside of this project under a separate Scope of Work and Professional Services quote." which means if it is not specifically mentioned here, you will pay for it somewhere down the line.

Write up every detail of every function you need and have the vendor include them in the Functional Specification. Pass it by your IT department for their input because it will affect them too. Say "this system will perform these following functions". If you don't ask for it now in writing, they will bill you for it later. For example, if you need two-sided scanning of your documents, make sure that is included.

Have IT highly involved during installation and training periods. The vendor's tech rep will need to come to install the software and train the IT people on the administration of it. Your IT people must have the hardware ready for the installation.

Have IT pre-order any items of hardware and software they need to support and grow the system. Usually your internal IT department wants to order the hardware so they can use their own vendors, track the hardware for maintenance, financial and security reasons. The vendor should give you a list of all the hardware and software they will need for their system to work.

Read the specifications of the recommended hardware. One hardware vendor suggested we buy a top-of-the-line printer that would print paper up to 17 inches wide and was of a brand different from any our company owned. We would have had to buy ink cartridges specifically for that printer, at a higher cost, then buying cartridges in bulk for the brand the company used. And we will probably never print anything wider than 11 inches. We settled for a model from the brand we already had in house.

What amount of internal computer memory is needed by any additional hardware? We purchased a scanner that was rated to scan 57 pages per minute, if our computer had a certain amount of memory. It didn't. So our scanning was slower than we wanted, until our IT department ordered and installed the extra memory on that computer.

The scanner was also scanning at a much slower rate than the vendor said it would. The vendor said it was networking problems, which is rather hard to believe when it was directly attached to the computer with the software installed. So while the vendor and IT sent emails back and forth, I explored the scanner set-up functions and found it was set to scan at the slowest rate available. Changing that setting more than doubled the speed of scanning.

Work closely with the vendor during installation and training periods to settle any details. The more you are involved, the more likely it is you will notice, find, and settle any issues that may grow into problems later.

One item I noticed right away was that the system did not let you delete an item and then add another item with the same unique identification number. So when the database was populated with records from an Excel spreadsheet (the old inventory method) and it was discovered the importation of data was incorrect and those records deleted, then the next import started numbering records from that point on. This means we do not have any records numbered 1 to 162. Not life threatening but just annoying not to have all sequential records starting from zero.

Make sure that you or a company IT person has administrator rights to all files within the software. One vendor installed a system with scheduled tasks. I was not given administrator rights to modify those scheduled tasks, which caused a problem when our needs changed. So I had to contact our IT department, which modified the rights on those files to enable me to re-schedule them.

Good rapport is needed between you, your IT department and the support system the vendor supplies. If you have it, everyone will respect each other and problems will get fixed quickly. If you do not have it, problems may take forever as each group complains and blames the other.

The vendor will ask you to sign off on the Functional Specification sheet right after the system is installed. Don't sign until all the functions you requested are installed and are working. You could write up a sheet saying that the system was installed and is working and give that to the vendor. Once you sign the Functional Spec sheet they could say you accepted the system and could charge you for any additional work.

Chapter 18 - Roll Out System to Company

After the system was installed and I had entered a number of documents and scanned their images into the system, I would invite the specific individuals from a department who would be working with that department's documents to view the system. I would explain how it worked and ask them how they wanted it customized for their use. Working together, we would develop the functions useful for them and start entering their documents. Soon, they were well enough trained to enter everything on their own.

Have user training sessions taught either by a vendor representation or, after your training as system administration, by you. You should draft up a short training session to use as a refresher course or for training new employees and draft up a full training session for a periodical training course for all employees.

Create your own in-house training sessions – you will learn by teaching the system as well as gain respect from company employees. I found it worked best to have small group sessions consisting of individuals from the same department. They could focus on the features important to them, and I did not have to remember all of the system functions, just what they needed to know.

Write down all questions that come up after installation and during the first 45 to 90 day period and contact vendor support to have those questions answered. You usually have a support period after installation that you should use for anything that comes up.

Put the vendor support telephone number in your system on speed-dial.

We had the software installed on two systems separate from one another, one inside our Library and another outside at my work area. After one month, we noticed that modifications we did on one machine did not show up on the other. It seems the software saved the settings locally, and not to the network, which would have shared the modifications with both machines. We called the vendor and had them fix it.

Write down and keep track of all questions, curious workings and glitches seen during the first year of operation because you may be able to get them answered or fixed when the second year of maintenance comes up for renewal

Especially write down users statements of "gee, it would be great if the system did…." and send those comments to tech support regularly. After six months of use, I had a two page list of questions and suggestions for improvements which I sent to the company. They thanked me but I am still waiting for some of those improvements to appear on the system.

Epilogue

End users resist change. There were several groups in OUR Company which had the system rolled out for their use, used it for a while and then ignored it. Why? They either resisted changing their business process or were just lazy. Our legal department wanted the system to scan in contracts. This would allow the legal and finance departments to quickly pull up a contract to check dates, payment amounts and payment schedules. I set up the system and scanned in the initial batch of contracts. They loved it. But week after week went by without legal sending me any new contracts. So I set up administrative rights and taught a legal admin how to enter records and scan in the contracts. They did not do this on a regular basis. And two years later they paid for an outside service to scan all of their invoices and contracts so they are paying for a service they could do in-house at no cost to the company.

Would I recommend this specific software system? **NO**.

VENDOR #2 was a local office supply company who realized in the 1980s that they should have some sort of document management software system so they went out and licensed one to sell. The software company which originated the system has a very small technical support group, which replied to us at their own very slow rate of speed.

VENDOR #2 does not use the system enough to be of any help. They are more interested in selling technical support for other products than supporting the one we purchased. They listen to my questions or emails, and forward them on to the corporate headquarters support group to be answered.

The headquarter company claimed to supply two updates a year. There was only one in the first three years we had the software.

The company uses its own specific labels for its label maker and does not sell them through any third parties. So I redesigned the labels to print on any label available from any supply source.

VENDOR #1, who was not chosen, sent me more emails asking how everything is going than the local support personnel. That says a lot about their customer service.

But hey, the VP of IT made the decision to purchase this software from VENDOR #2 while I was advocating for the software from VENDOR #1. So whenever anyone complained, I just told them it was his choice and his fault.

I hope sharing this history will help others doing computer software evaluation.

Thank you,
Dale Carpenter

Bibliography

I apologize for the incompleteness of this bibliography. The articles were gathered and compiled over several decades as I saw their relevance to work I was doing at the time. It was only when I came to write this bibliography that I noticed a number of the articles did not have complete publication data on them.

I have tried searching online for the exact publication information of these articles. I have found some but others still remain hidden. For example, the M. K. Badawy columns from Machine Design could not be found on the Machine Design website (www.machinedesign.com). The Kate Ludeman article can be found on the Machine Design website. So perhaps the other columns are so old they have not been scanned yet.

This issue makes me wonder how easy it will be to find articles or publications solely electronic in nature years after the original publication date. But discussing that issue is a subject for another book.

The public and private communications referred to were either vocal in nature or in emails which happened so long ago I did not go to the trouble of searching for them even if the emails were available to me. However the kernels of wisdom imparted to me have been incorporated into this book. I hope they are helpful to you also.

Abram, Stephen. "Beyond Elevator Speeches! A Process for Influence". (November 2006). *Information Outlook.* Vol. 10, No. 11, p50. www.sla.org.

Abram, Stephen. "Committing to Innovation: No Excuses". (July/August 2009). *Information Outlook.* Vol. 13, No. 5. p47. www.sla.org.

Abram, Stephen. "Competing With Google in a Special Library". (November 2005). *Information Outlook.* Vol. 9, No. 11. p46. www.sla.org.

Abram, Stephen. "Dressing Up and Taking Our Show On The Road". (April 2003). *Information Outlook.* p23. www.sla.org.

Abram, Stephen. "Earning the Right to an Opinion Requires Real-World Experience". (May 2007). *Information Outlook.* Vol. 11, No. 5. p50. www.sla.org.

Abram, Stephen. "How Can We Make Innovation Spread Through Our Organizations?". (September 2007). *Information Outlook.* Vol. 11, No. 9. p38. www.sla.org.

Abram, Stephen. "Is There Such a Thing as Information Overload?". (February 2008). *Information Outlook.* Vol. 12, No. 2. p25 www.sla.org.

Abram, Stephen. "Politics and Research: To Run a Campaign, You Can't Have One Without the Other". (August 2007). *Information Outlook*. Vol. 11, No. 8. p36. www.sla.org.

Abram, Stephen. "Preparing For Change in Technology and the Economy". (November 2008). *Information Outlook*. Vol. 12, No. 11. p48. www.sla.org.

Abram, Stephen. "Tips to Boost Innovation for You and Your Library: Parts 1, 2 & 3". (August, September & October 2005). *Information Outlook*. Vol. 9, No. 8 (p32), 9 (p40) & 10 (p44). www.sla.org.

Abram, Stephen. "Why Should I Care About Standards?". (March 2003). *Information Outlook*. p21. www.sla.org.

Abram, Stephen. Lessons From the Past Require Preservation". (November 2004). *Information Outlook*. Vol. 8, No. 11. p42. www.sla.org.

Abram, Stephen." Strategic Questions For Future Planning". (October/November 2010). *Information Outlook*. Vol. 14, No. 7. p37. www.sla.org.

Abramo, Dean. Logistics Manager. Public and private communications.

Affelt, Amy. "Aligning the Information Center to Create the Future". (June 2009). *Information Outlook*. Vol. 13, No. 4. p33. www.sla.org.

Ainsbury, Bob and Futornick, Michelle. "The Revenge of the Library Scientist". (November 2000). *Online*. www.onlineinc.com.

Akst, Daniel. "Information Liberation". (March 7, 2008). *The Wall Street Journal*. pW13.

Augustyniak, Rebecca; Finley, Amy; Aguero, Dawn; Monroe, Blair; & Arsenault, Brian. "The Information Professional's Role in Creating Business Management Systems". (September 2005). *Information Outlook*. Vol. 9, No. 9. p12. www.sla.org.

Badawy, M. K. "How To Manage Your Boss". (?). *Machine Design*. p236. www.machinedesign.com.

Badawy, M. K. "Making Time Work For You". (?). *Machine Design*. p228. www.machinedesign.com.

Balas, Janet L. "Adding Substance, Not Just Frills, To a Library's Online Catalog". (March 2004). *Computers in Libraries*. Vol. 24, No. 3. www.infotoday.com.

Basefsky, Stewart. "The Personal Information Trainer". (November 2007). *Information Outlook*. Vol. 11, No. 11. p11. www.sla.org.

Batts, Sarah. "Strategies and Tactics for Workplace Research". (January/February 2011). *Information Outlook*. Vol. 15, No. 1. p27. www.sla.org.

Beasom, Shawn. Linguist and world traveler. Private and public communications.

Beasom, William T. ("Buck"). Financial wizard. Private and public communications.

Binder, Carl. "Measurement Counts! Projecting Trends, Or How I Got A New Consulting Gig". (June 2003). www.performancexpress.org

Bingham, Tony. "Aligning Learning with Organizational Results". (September 2010). *Information Outlook*. Vol. 14, No. 6. p10. www.sla.org.

Brandon Hall Research. "Learning C-Speak: The Language of Executives". (2006). www.brandon–hall.com.

Brockmann, Eric N. and Anthony, William P. "Tactic Knowledge and Strategic Decision-making". (December 2002). *Group and Organizational Management*. Vol. 27, No. 4. p436.

Bromley, Marilyn. "Return On Investment". Quantum2 Case Study 3.04.02. Dialog, A Thompson Company.

Canby, Susan Fifer. "Strategies for Climbing the Corporate Ladder". (May 2005). *Information Outlook*. Vol. 9, No. 5. p13. www.sla.org.

Carpenter, Lynn. Custom Building and Remodeling. Private and public communications.

Chapman, Janet L. "The Information Scientist as Database Manager in a Corporate Environment". (Spring 1986). *Special Libraries*. p71.

Chmelik, Samantha. "Market Research for Libraries". (February 2006). *Information Outlook*. Vol. 10, No. 2. p23. www.sla.org.

Cohen, Allan R. "The Illusion of Authority, The Centrality of Influence". (March 2010). *Information Outlook*. Vol. 14, No. 2. p17. www.sla.org.

Colton, Stephanie and Ward, Victoria. "Story as a Tool to Capitalize on Knowledge Assets". (2004). *Business Information Review*. Vol. 21, No. 3. p172.

Cooke, Walter. "An Expert on a Disk: Automating Data Classification Work Using Expert Systems". (May 1994). Sixth Annual Canadian Computer Security Symposium, Ottawa, Canada.

Coronato, Patrick. Engineer. Public and private communications.

Curran, Charles. "What Do Librarians and Information Scientists Do?". (January 2001). *American Libraries*. Vol. 32, Issue 1. p56. Americanlibrariesmagazine.org.

Davenport, Thomas H. "Putting the I in IT". (August 7, 2002). *The Financial Times*.

Davenport, Thomas H., Prusak, Lawrence; and Strong, Bruce. "Putting Ideas to Work: Knowledge Management Can Make a Difference - But It

Needs to Be More Pragmatic". (March 10, 2008). *The Wall Street Journal.* pR11.

Davies, Kevin. "Search and Deploy". (October 2006). *BIO IT World.* p24. www.bio–itworld.com.

Dimattia, Susan S. "A Gem of a Plan: Gemological Institute of America Recovery Plan Sets Procedures for 50 Different Disasters". (June 2007). *Information Outlook.* Vol. 11, No. 6. p27. www.sla.org.

Dinerman, Gloria. "If You Don't Know, Ask: The Art and Craft of Survey". (July 2002). *Information Outlook.* p6. www.sla.org.

Dobson, Chris. "Beyond the Information Audit: Checking the Health of an Organization's Information System". (July/August 2002). *Searcher.* Vol. 10, No. 7. www.infotoday.com.

Doering, William. "Managing the Transition to a New Library Catalog: Tips For Smooth Sailing". (July/August 2000). *Computers in Libraries.* Vol. 20, No. 7. www.infotoday.com.

Donovan, Hedley. "Managing Your Intellectuals". (October 23, 1989). *Fortune.* p177.

Dove, Rick "The Knowledge Worker". (June 1998). *Automotive Manufacturing and Production.* www.parshift.com. Agility Essay #42.

Dysart, Jane and Abram, Stephen. "Time Management and the Special Librarian". (October 1990). *Specialist; The Newsletter of Special Libraries Association.* Vol. 13, No. 10. p5.

Eastman, Cynthia. "Overcoming the Curse of Knowledge: Communicating the Library's Value". (January/February 2010). *Information Outlook.* Vol. 14, No. 1. p37. www.sla.org.

Eddison, Elizabeth Bole. "Who Should Be in Charge?". (April 1983). *Special Libraries.* p107.

Enterprise Tracking Systems Corporation. "Buyer's Guide: Top Questions to Ask When Purchasing Software". www.enterprisetracker.com.

Fisher, Donna M. "Flying Solo? Involve Your Patrons in Your Work; Involve Your Library in Theirs". (?) *Flying Solo.* p23. www.solo.sla.org.

Galligan, Sarah. "The Information Resources Specialist as Group Facilitator in an Organizational Setting". (Fall 1985). *Special Libraries.* p246.

Garshol, Lars Marius. "Metadata? Thesauri? Taxonomies? Topic maps! Making Sense of it All". (August 2004). *Journal of Information Science.* Vol. 30, No. 4. p378.

Gasaway, Laura. "Drafting An Organizational Copyright Policy". (2004?). *Information Outlook.* p36. www.sla.org.

Goman, Carol Kinsey. "Forces of Change". (May 2004). *Information Outlook.* p34. www.sla.org.

Grenny, Joseph. "Five Crucial Conversations for Successful Projects". (August 2007). *Quality Digest.* p26. www.qualitydigest.com.

Guevara, Sophia. "Proactive Marketing: Connecting With the Corporate Client". (February 2008). *Information Outlook.* Vol. 12, No. 2. p21. www.sla.org.

Head, Alison J. "Web Redemption and The Promise of Usability". (November–December 1999). *Online.* Vol. 23, Issue 6. p21.

Henczel, Sue. "Supporting the KM Environment: The Roles, Responsibilities, and Rights of Information Professionals". (January 2004). *Information Outlook.* p14. www.sla.org.

Henczel, Susan. "The Information Audit as a First Step Towards Effective Knowledge Management". (June 2001). *Information Outlook.* Vol. 5, No. 6. www.sla.org.

Hill, Linda L. "Rosabeth Moss Kanter Speaks at the SLA Boston Conference, June 9, 1986". (Fall 1986). *Special Libraries.* p235.

Hook, Sarah Anne. "Management Insight: Communicating With a Non-Librarian Boss". (Spring 1995). *Library Management Quarterly.* Vol. 18, No. 2. p6.

IBM. "IBM Ease-of-Use – Web Design Guidelines Section" (November 9, 2001) www.IBM.com.

Information Management Associates, Inc. "An Information Management Needs Inventory". (2004). www.informat.org.

Information Management Associates, Inc. "Records Retention Schedules: More Than The Law". (2004). www.informat.org.

Information Today, Inc. "Best Practices in Records Management & Regulatory Compliance" (September 2003). Supplement to *KMworld.*

International Society for Performance Improvement. "ISPI's Performance Technology Standards". (2002). www.ispi.org.

J. Morelli Consulting Ltd. "A Guide to Retention Scheduling". (December 2000). *Record Management Society (UK) Bulletin.* Issue 100.

J. Morelli Consulting Ltd. "Process-driven Retention Scheduling". (December 1999). *Records Management Society (UK) Bulletin.* Issue 94.

James, Sylvia. "Valuing Business Information Services: Calculating Base Costs, Premia and Discounts to Demonstrate the Benefits They Offer". (2004). *Business Information Review.* Vol. 21, No. 3. p157.

Jarche, Harold. "Personal Knowledge Management: Working and Learning Smarter". (September 2010). *Information Outlook*. Vol. 14, No. 6. p13. www.sla.org.

Kennedy, Mary Lee and Abell, Angela. "New Roles for Info Pros". (January 2008). *Information Outlook*. Vol. 12, No. 1. p25. www.sla.org.

Kiechel III, Walter. "In Praise of Office Gossip". (August 19, 1985). *Fortune*. p253.

Kimball, Ralph. "Data Warehouse Designer: An Engineer's View". (July 26, 2002). www.intelligententerprise.com. p20.

Kotter, John P. "How To Save Good Ideas". (October 2010). *Harvard Business Review*. p129.

Latham, John R. "Value Your Activities Early, Often to Keep Management Informed". (January 2008). *Information Outlook*. Vol. 12, No. 1. p44. www.sla.org.

Launt, Geoffrey. Engineer. Public and private communications.

Leibowitz, Jay, Rubenstein–Montano, Bonnie, McCaw, Doug, Buchwalter, Judah and Browning, Chuck. "The Knowledge Audit". (2004). Department of Information Systems, University of Maryland – Baltimore County.

Leigh, Doug. "Worthy Performance, Redux". (June 2003). www.performancexpress.org.

Little, Anne and Millington, Kathleen. "Enabling End-User Shopping on Our Corporate Library's Intranet". (September 2001). Vol. 21, No. 8. *Computers in Libraries*. www.infotoday.com.

Loeb, Marshall. "How To Make the CEO Buy Your idea". (December 11, 1995). *Fortune*. p210.

Ludeman, Kate. "Letting Go of Lost Causes". (May 24, 1984). *Machine Design*. p170. www.machinedesign.com.

Matthews, Joseph R. "Determining and Communicating the Value of the Special Library". (March 2003). *Information Outlook*. p26. www.sla.org.

McAlister, James. "Preparing A Persuasive Proposal". (February 21, 1985). *Machine Design*. p129. www.machinedesign.com.

Mehta, Samir "Sam". Computer hardware and software expert. Private and public communications.

Mitchell, David. Computer hardware and software expert. Private and public communications.

Moseley, Marty. "Simplifying Master Data Management Deployments". (June 2009). *Database Trends and Applications*. p12.

Moulton, Lynda W. "The Procurement Process: Making Major Purchases for Corporate Libraries". (June 10, 1991). Presentation Handout from Special Libraries Association Conference, San Antonio, Texas.

Murray, Art. "Goodbye, Knowledge Worker... Hello, Knowledge Entrepreneur". (June 2008). KM world. p20. www.kmworld.com.

Nielsen, Jakob and Sano, Darrel. "1994 Design of SunWeb - Sun Microsystems' Intranet". www.nngroup.com.

Nielsen, Tom. "Four Steps I Took That Transformed My Solo Corporate Library". (September/October 2002). *Marketing Library Services.* Vol. 16, No. 6/7. www.infotoday.com.

Nordan, Ken. "When Your Organization Can't Get a KM Project Started, Take It Personally!". (March 2005). *Information Outlook.* Vol. 9, No. 3. p17. www.sla.org.

Pantry, Sheila, and Griffiths, Peter. "Changing for the Better: Is Your Reputation at Stake?" (2004). *Business Information Review.* Vol. 21, No. 3. p165.

Phillips, Jeff and Klima, Christine. "Overcoming Information Overload". (May 2004). *Transform.* www.transformmag.com.

Pollock, Ted. "Mine Your Own Business: The Gentle Art of Selling Change". (December 2000). S*upervision.* Vol. 61, Is. 12. p11.

Pringer, Tim. Computer hardware and software expert. Private and public communications.

Regional Resource and Federal Center Network Information Specialists. "Just Ask: The Best Way to Get Your Clients the Right Information is to Find Out Exactly What They Want". (April 2006). *Information Outlook.* Vol. 10, No. 4. p33. www.sla.org.

Ries, Al and Trout, Jack. "Butchering the Sacred Cows: Top-down Marketing Strategy No Longer Works". (February 6, 1989). *Industry Week.* p27.

Rinehart, Mitzi M. "How to Survive in a Downsizing Environment". (August 1993). *Sci-Tech News.* p14.

Ryan, Terry. "Turning Patrons into Partners When Choosing an Integrated Library System". (March 2004). *Computers in Libraries.* Vol. 24, No. 3. p6. www.infotoday.com.

Sanderson, Martin and Ward, Sandra. "Records Management Mission Critical". (August 2003). *Library + Information Update.* www.cilip.org.uk.

Saporito, Bill. "The Revolt Against 'Working Smarter'". (July 21, 1986). *Fortune.* p58.

Schachter, Debbie. "Relationship and Network Building". (May 2006). *Information Outlook*. Vol. 10, No. 5. p10. www.sla.org.

Scott, Donald. "Evaluating Products: Finding the Right Solution for You". (December 2003). Vol. 5, No. 3. *AIIM E-DOC Magazine*. www.aiim.org.

Scotty, George J. "Proving Value and Return On Investment". (June 2010). *Information Outlook*. Vol. 14, No. 4. p22. www.sla.org.

Serbin, Joseph Economic Development Specialist. Public and private communications.

Sherman, Will. "33 Reasons Why Libraries and Librarians are Still Extremely Important" (2007). *Information Outlook*. Vol. 11, No. 6. p67. www.sla.org.

Simon, Carol. "How Can You Be a Manager? You're a Solo!" (March 2005). *Information Outlook*. Vol. 9, No. 3. p13. www.sla.org.

Smith, David Y. and Waddington, Tad. "Running Training Like a Business: Determining the Return on Investment of Your Learning Programs". (February 2003). *Outlook Point of View*. www.accenture.com.

Special Libraries Association. "Higher Ranked Fortune 500 Companies Significantly More Likely to Have Libraries". (March 2000). *Information Outlook*. p12. www.sla.org.

Special Libraries Association. "What Is The Cost of Misinformation? An Executive Summary from *"Exploring Outsourcing: Case Studies of Corporate Libraries"*". (April 21, 1997). www.sla.org.

Special Libraries Association's Library Management Division and Advertising & Marketing Division Presentation. "Expanding Your Influence Beyond the Library". (June 12, 1991). *Library Management Quarterly*. Vol. 14, No. 3, Spring 1991. p9.

Standish Group International, The. "Success/Failure Profiles" (1995). Standishgroup.com

Strand, Jill. "Strike Up the Brand: How to Market Your Value to The Rest of The World". (May 2004). *Information Outlook*. p11. www.sla.org.

Strouse, Roger. "Demonstrating Value and Return on Investment: The Ongoing Imperative". (March 2003). *Information Outlook*. p14. www.sla.org.

Thompson, Sara R. and Geohring, George L. "Engineering Our Own Library Catalog". (February 2001). *Computers in Libraries*. Vol. 21, No. 2. www.infotoday.com.

Tomaiuolo, Nicholas G. "Playing Twenty Questions to Test Low-Cost, Free, or Subscription Databases for End-User Online Service". (May 2001). *Searcher*. Vol. 9, No. 5. www.infotoday.com.

Usual cast of corporate management idiots, The. Various companies I've worked at. Public and private communications.

Vales, Joe and Vales, Kerry Ann. "Knowledge Management Drives Corporate Sustainability". (January/February 2006). *HRO Today*. p14.

Viele, Pat. "How Do We Serve Thee? Let Us Count the Ways". (September 2005). *Information Outlook*. Vol. 9, No. 9. p19. www.sla.org.

Wagner, Pat. "The Three Skills You Need to Have for Successful Project Management". (August 2006). *Information Management*. Vol. 10, No. 8. p24.

Werts, Cybele Elaine. "Technology as a Catalyst for Personal and Organizational Change". (June 2007). *Information Outlook*. Vol. 11, No. 6. p55. www.sla.org.

White, Herbert S. "Special Libraries and the Corporate Political Process". (April 1984). *Special Libraries*. p81.

Wilson, Barbara S., Freeman, Elizabeth, and Grimshaw, Jeff. "Piercing the "Wall of Ignorance": A Communication Strategy for an Information Center". (November 2003). *Information Outlook*. p22. www.sla.org.

Zach, Lisl. "A Librarian's Guide to Speaking the Business Language". (June 2002). *Information Outlook*. p18. www.sla.org.

Zipperer, Lorri and Thompson, Sara. "Systems Thinking: A New Avenue for Involvement and Growth". (November 2006). *Information Outlook*. Vol. 10, No. 11. p16. www.sla.org.

INDEX

Thanks for buying this book. I hope it was helpful.

If you think it was, please help pass the information on by:

Recommending this book to friends, co-workers or anyone you think might find it useful.

Write about this book on your social account, or book review sites such as Goodbooks.

Tell everyone in the professional societies you belong to, especially the book reviewers.

You can also help me by emailing me at:
LiesToldPress@mail.com,
And telling me:

How could I have made it better?

Was there a question you wanted me to answer that went unanswered?

How was the amount of detail in the book? Did you want less or more? And where and why?

Were you inspired or motivated in some way?

Thanks. By doing this you will improve the future editions of this book and all other books I write.

Lies Told Press, LTD. is a non-profit company helping authors and artists publish and market their works. All profits, except for what is needed to keep us running, go directly back to the authors and artists. Lies Told Press, LTD. books are available at www.Lulu.com.

www.ingramcontent.com/pod-product-compliance
Lightning Source LLC
Chambersburg PA
CBHW051245050326
40689CB00007B/1068